JAMES COLLINS

James Collins was born in England during t
Masters degree and has taught theatre and
musicals, all performed in the United Kingdom, and has worked on the cabaret circuit. He moved to the warmer climate of Greece in 2002 and has been happily writing novels ever since.

Also by James Collins

Other people's dreams

You wish

Into the fire

Jason and the Sargonauts

Carry on up the Kali Strata

These novels are available in paperback and hardback
Details at www.symidream.com

Copyright © James Collins 2006

Some of the content contained in Symi 85600 has appeared on the website www.symidream.com – a website about life on Symi, Greece written material by James Collins and Neil Gosling.

Drawings by James

SYMI 85600

James Collins

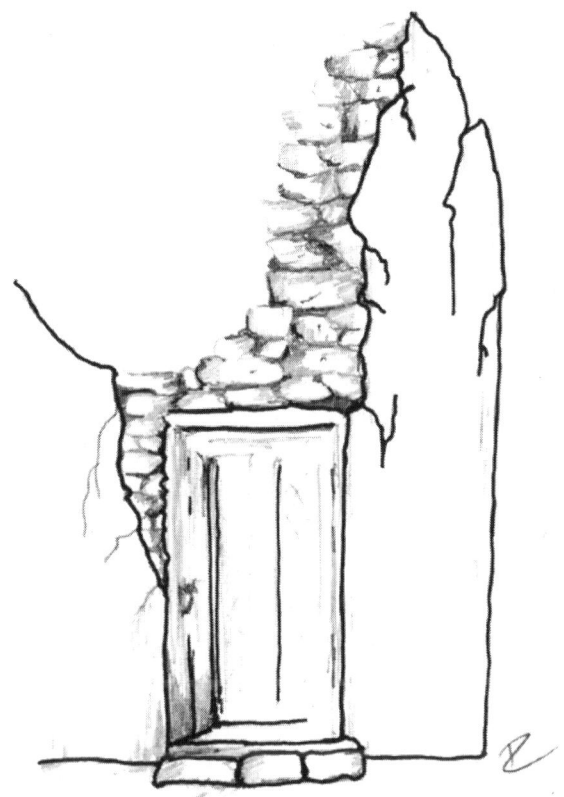

For my mother
Who is a much better artist than me.

INTRODUCTIONS

Hi.

I am writing this to you from a 19th century building that has been a house with no toilet, a butcher's shop, a barber's and a jewellery shop. Now it is a digital photo shop. As I type on my Logitech keyboard pausing occasionally to download customers' images from their mobile phones to CDs, a train of mules passes by carrying wooden scaffolding and rocks. The old lady who lives next door pops in occasionally with homemade biscuits to chatter in a dialect I will never understand while a group of ex-pats drink gin and Tonic outside the nearby bar gossiping in a language I understand only too well. In the summer months the temperature climbs to, and stays in, the high forties and in the winter I sit and work in gloves and a heavy overcoat.

Welcome to Symi, Dodecanese, Greece.

There were so many television programmes selling the idyllic idea of leaving the United Kingdom and living a dream life in the sun that we just had to do it, if only to get away from them.

And so we did. On August 28th 2002 we left Brighton, hung around at Stanstead airport for a while and finally arrived in Athens at six thirty, local time.

Four years later and I have decided that it is time you had a first hand insight into what it is actually like to sell up and live your dream.

The following pages contain small articles and notes that, in the main, I have written for the website, www.symidream.com. I have included a set of monthly e-mails we sent to friends 'back home' during our first year as these give an honest account of what we were doing and feeling at the time and were not written with a commercial venture in mind. And, at the end of the book, I have included a handy little section called 'How to move to a Greek island, or other place in the sun.' This first appeared as an e-book in 2004 and, so readers tell me, is useful for anyone thinking of moving abroad, not necessarily to Greece. It's also quite amusing they say.

But first some background…

Getting here

Neil and I first came to Symi on holiday in August 1998. As we were ferried into the amphitheatre of neoclassical architecture which is the harbour and main town we had no idea that this small island off the coat of Turkey would one day be our home.

Cut to:

Four years later.

Leaving England on the afternoon of our fifth anniversary we arrived in Athens at the height of smog season, August. We left two days later having seen as many sites and sights as we thought polite and headed south by boat. Our original idea was to island hop while searching out a suitable venue to call home for our trial year as ex-pats. In previous years we had visited Lefkada, Patmos, Leros, Kalymnos, Kos (for three hours) and Symi. I had also made a solo tour of Skiathos and Skopolos in years gone by but the Dodecanese was always my favourite island chain. We headed, therefore, straight to Paros which is actually in the Cyclades but neither of us had been there and I'd read a book about it once so it seemed a good idea.

A few hours after leaving Piraeus we landed on Paros and a few minutes after landing on Paros we were in the back of a Land Rover heading to some apartments owned by someone's brother's wife's cousin. But even Paros, by our 'looking for somewhere small and quiet' standards was too big and so the customary two days later we were off again to the nearby and smaller Antiparos. Before we had even stepped onto the ferry we had had accommodation secured for us by some chap who had a relative who had a nice place for us to stay so we were quite impressed by Greek efficiency. At this point - wait until later! The place couldn't have been better; a self contained studio with a kitchen, balcony and view and only a clothes' throw away from one of the few licensed nudist beaches in Greece.

We stayed five days on Antiparos. No it wasn't the lure of the nudist beach though I did wander down there one morning at sunrise and looked across the water. There was nothing in sight to suggest the 21st century, I could have been back in Homer's day looking at a landscape of sea and rock that would not change for centuries. Until the ice cream van came along and the family set up, getting ready to sell snacks to naked north Europeans.

We even went as far as to look for permanent accommodation though anything in our budget was scarce. We considered our work options, we had enough saved up for a winter without work but would need to find something the following summer. There was a school of English on the island and I considered applying to teach there, dreaming of fitting into the local community overnight while helping to bring enlightenment and culture to the island. Not to be.

Here's a thing I've noticed: Many, if not most, potential (and even some fully fledged) ex-pats I've come to know and avoid have had the romantic notion that no one in Greece speaks English and that anyone who is English can teach it. Wrong! Most Greek people (particularly the younger generations) speak English, many speak it better than some English people I know and to teach it you must have more of a qualification than just being English. So if you're thinking of escaping the rat race to live abroad and think you'll teach English for some extra cash, my advice is to get qualified and prepare to be out of work.

You would be better off learning Greek and teaching it to the English.

We decided to leave Antiparos, charming though it and its people were, because it was too small, had a limited tourist season in which to earn a year's supply of money and it was too flat for Neil. Being a photographer and keen walker he needs hills to make his life mean something. After five days he felt he had photographed everything there was for him on the island - nudist beach excepted.

So, in the end, we were drawn back to Symi. We'd been here before, we knew a few people and we had secretly fallen for the place on that first visit four years earlier. So decision made we booked our passage. After a sleepless night in deck class on the ferry Marina, (whoever nicked my sleeping mat I hope you never have a good night's sleep again) we finally arrived on Rhodes on the afternoon of Neil's thirty fifth birthday. At least being awake all night meant that he saw the sun come up over Kalymnos on his big day. Even more finally we arrived on Symi at three thirty in the afternoon carrying two large rucksacks (one without sleeping mat), two small rucksacks and a lap top.

We were here to stay. We were ready for rural Greek living. Island life. Back to basics.

Two years later we would have a large rented house with garden, terrace and balcony, a real fire, indoor bathroom, large TV, DVD player, video, three mobile phones, four computers, two cats and a piano.

E-Mails to friends

September 2002
Dear Lisa and Christina

We are staying on Symi and have found a house. It is right up at the top of the village, about 500 steps and half an hour's walk from the harbour. But it has spectacular views, plenty of room and two courtyards. We are sharing it with someone until she moves out in October and then it will be ours for, hopefully, a whole year or more.

It was good of you to see us off on the second stage of our journey. We were told the ferry left Paros at midnight but, as we sat down at eleven for a last drink we saw it pull in. We made it with only seconds to spare! The voyage was both hard work and pleasant. We sat under the stars, tried to sleep on the floor, watched the sun rise on Neil's birthday, saw several islands from a distance, sailed past Symi so close that we could have touched it and arrived at Rhodes fourteen hours after we left Paros. We then had a long walk with all our bags and a short wait for a hydrofoil, finally arriving on Symi at 3.30 pm on Sunday. We got into our booked apartment at 8 pm! Quite a day! Neil has started working already and I have spent the two weeks searching for this house, which we now have, so I can start to relax and think about writing again.

The season will end in about six weeks and then we will both have time together. At the moment we only see each other for a couple of hours a day, as Neil works from 5 pm to 1 am and then has his 'evening' at the bar etc. while I sleep. Sometimes we have had breakfast together at 5.30 am – he has an ouzo and I have cereal!

Dear Nigel

I am writing this the night before I go down to the harbour to check the e-mails so it may cross with any message you've sent recently.

Thanks for the text – I still dislike mobile phones but they are handy. Last night I texted Neil to ask him to get some anti-mosquito supplies as I was being bitten to death. (Still look like the elephant man.) A little later and half the people in the bar with him were texting me with advice and suggestions. There are no secrets here.

We have moved into 'Villa Skilaki' as we call it, skilaki being Greek for Neil's nick-name 'puppy' and everything so far is fine up here. You MUST book a flight or holiday soon as I am sure it's going to be a popular destination next year. (Symi as well as our house.) Apparently Symi is going to be featured on a holiday programme in the spring and Spielberg is shooting a film here sometime so it could become another Kefalonia*. In fact now might be a good time to buy, I'd love to buy this place but I don't think the landlord wants to sell it, he's planning to retire here in a couple of years.

Regards to Mother!

* The British holiday programme 'Wish you were here?' did feature Symi in 2004 but as yet (2006) no sign of Mr. Spielberg, although a Greek drama series and a Turkish soap opera have both recently been filmed here.

October 2002

Dear Diva

Thank you for the mail which had the whole internet café in stitches. I expect it will be appearing in the local paper, the Athens News (in Greek) and on various web pages by next week. You'll be pleased to hear that we have secured a villa with enough space to accommodate a diva and her trunks (Vuiton, swimming and otherwise.) So you can organise your diary for next year and book in to 'Villa Skilaki', but be prepared for a long climb. Superb views from the salon roof, just below the highest church (noisy when the bells go off) and set among some ruins like something from a gothic novel. But it does have sleeping space for about six, plus the salon for those who can sleep on the floor.

I have already lost about half a stone and can almost see my feet again. The diet is mainly veg, fruit, pasta and Ouzo and the exercise involved in climbing up to the house through the alleyways and ruins is helping. Neil's schedule means that he works from 5.30 pm until about one, and often goes with Amanda to the late night bar, getting home at around three. He's often not in bed until five and I don't really see him until mid day. By then I've done the washing, milked the goats, been to church, said my rosary, worn out my black frock and filled the well. A bit odd but am getting used to it. The season will be over in a few weeks and, if the weather gets windy or wet before then, his job will finish sooner as the Windmill is all outside seating.

Talking of weather, after a couple of days of wind and a poor attempt at rain one night, we're now back up in the 80s, very hot but the nights are cooling down. I'm as usual covered with mosquito bites and have a face like John Merrick, feet like balloons and a left elbow which people come miles to gawp at.

Enough babble.

Thank Alistair for the message about the dreaded Rhodes. I went there last week to buy us the mobile phones, since when Neil has done nothing but text people rude jokes, but at least Rhodes has shops. Alistair would much more enjoy Symi I think though 'Frog' might not like the steps, stony beaches and toilet facilities – we flush with the shower bowl or washing up water as this house has a history of water shortage and, although Thursday is 'water day' when a little old man wanders around turning on your feed and you have to check it's coming through the hose pipe across the courtyard and into the sterna, you never know how much, if any, you are going to get.

Sunday 24th November 2002
Dear All

Here is the November update from Symi for you to read at your leisure.

Today is Sunday 24th Nov. and, as I write, Neil is sunbathing in the courtyard, while also making marmalade with oranges from our tree and boiling up pasta to mix with dog food to feed to the stray cats who live at the bins in the village. That's a typical sort of Symi activity for a Sunday. No one day is ever the same as the last and so far this month we have done a variety of things:

Attended a bonfire/fireworks party at an ex-pat house, the small bonfire was among the ruins which is their back garden and was very atmospheric although the fireworks were a bit lame – the Greeks tend to save their explosives for Easter, New Year and election times when it's gunpowder, bombs and guns which provide the spectacle. We have met several non-Greek people some of whom live here all year round and others who are seasonal. Because you can't help being drawn into this small community you tend to make friends very quickly and at this time of year it is a round of dinner parties and lunches with 'your own kind'. Having said that we are slowly being recognised by the Greek folk and, as we are now both having Greek lessons with local Greek teachers, we are being more adventurous with our conversations and therefore providing much entertainment to the 'locals' with our misuse of the language.

We have attended the name day of Archangel Michael/Panormitis, followed the icon around the church, feasted at a monastery in the hills, lit candles and so on, being transported back and forth to these things in the back of an ancient transit van. The owners of the van came to us for lunch recently during which we were invited to launch someone's boat. We did that in the afternoon accompanied by a Kiwi, a plumber, a stray puppy and a dog called Todger.

We've visited the doctor to get cream for the roundworm our kittens have given us – sorted out now. The kittens are growing and provide hours of entertainment. Pipe is now almost twelve inches long and Slippers, who has long fur and looks like a Scottie Dog with crossed eyes, (she's half blind having been ill when little) is now almost a cat. Both are rescue cats but get on so well they could have come from the same plastic bag. (Pipe was found hanging in a carrier bag in a tree.) Neil's volunteered to help with the stray cat feeding programme during the winter which involves cooking pasta and dog food, taking it down to the village and feeding it to the strays.

We have also attended a housewarming party, several dinner parties and luncheons.

I have written a few articles, collected pebbles and stones for painting on (a new hobby of mine), drawn pictures, taken 100s of digital photos (Neil). Walked into the interior of the island and around the bays to see the ancient catacombs and Roman mosaic, watched DVDs at home, been swimming in the sea – in November, waved off many new friends returning to the UK (and other parts) for the winter, texted like mad, enquired about jobs – more news to follow when the jobs we want are confirmed. Played Pictionary and charades, watched the lightening across Turkey during a couple of thunder storms, got wet, got dry again, baked cakes in our now working oven, made marmalade with our own oranges. Started on a new novel. Oh, and Neil's been to Rhodes for photo supplies and encountered a hare with a shotgun – long story.

So life chugs on. We have a calendar on the wall now as it's necessary to keep track of all the things which fill the days – invites, lessons and so on. We keep saying that 'next week' we will have some free time and I can knuckle down to some work, uninterrupted for a few days, but it never seems to quite work that way and we're not complaining. Yesterday we went to the harbour to send emails and buy a TV guide. No emails were sent but we did get a lift home in a jeep, with shopping, a pan of lentil soup and a dog called Barbie. A quiet evening in consisted of a beer at the kafeneion, a debate on whether ours is an orange or mandarin tree (or a hybrid of both) and Harry Potter on DVD. Such is life on a small Greek island.

Christmas 2002
Dear All

Happy Christmas from this small Greek island. A small and rather chilly Greek island actually but we're getting used to that. During the day when the sun is out we can still manage a couple of hours in tee shirts but once it drops behind the mountain it's on with the jumpers, boots and sometimes gloves. And that's just to watch TV. We have a small heater we can huddle round and the cats keep us warm. Luckily we have a good heater in the bedroom so we can warm that room up before going to bed. Of course, when getting up early to walk the dog, the room is like an ice box but a quick scarper up the mountain and along the road with 'Barbie' soon heats us up. We take it in turns to walk Barbie. We are looking after her for a friend, she's an energetic dingo-looking thing who hates thunder but loves to run off and scour the island if we let her. Finding her again involves a long arduous search so we try to keep her on the lead unless we're out walking in the mountains.

The Greek lessons are progressing, me twice a week and Neil once a week. I try to learn at least one new word a day and find a way of using it the following day. Yesterday it was 'Sage' the herb Fascomilio and the day before 'cigarette papers' Harta, trying to fit both into the same sentence could prove a problem.

Many of the places providing internet connections are closed now, or only open at odd hours and most are down in the harbour where we tend to go only in the mornings and so sending regular emails will be difficult until things start up again next season – or until we get a phone line. Having said that a near neighbour has said we can use her machine and we'll try and be more punctual with replies and communications.

January 03 on Symi

It kind of started with a bang and went out with one actually. New Year's Eve, up on the roof, Neil's children rang up just before midnight which was great. As he was speaking to them the bells chimed across the island and a few pots of dynamite went off. The following night nature decided to have a go and we had the most ferocious thunderstorm I can remember. At one point, at around four in the morning, everyone was convinced that their house had been hit. It certainly sounded to us as though our church, not 50 metres away, had taken a direct strike. (I had – Neil woke with such a jolt that he head-butted me. Then Barbie got in to bed too but the crashing thunder made her shake with nerves poor thing and the shaking brought on her incontinence so I threw her out. It was like trying to sleep with a noisy washing machine on its final spin cycle.) It turned out to be the church of Stavros that had been hit, about 100 metres away, and there is now a chunk missing from its courtyard wall. The storm blew up half of the televisions on the island and several people lost their phones and computers to an electrical surge. Luckily our laptop survived as did Jennifer's TV that we are borrowing, although our landlord's old one needs a visit to the TV hospital in Pedi.

Time generally seems to be passing quickly and in only eight weeks I will be 40. In about 12 weeks the season will start again and winter will seem like it passed by in a flash. (Of lightning maybe?) Things seem to take more time here, or we take more time to do them. A trip to the harbour to check the mail can take up to four hours once we've walked down, fed cats, had our morning coffee by the quay, chatted, walked back and done the shopping en route. And only last week we had a nine hour lunch with some new friends. When Jane returned and we drove Barbie-dog down to meet the boat at four pm, Neil didn't arrive back home until after three the next morning having invented a new dance in a Kafeneion, had a peanut fight and left articles of clothing in a bar…

Greek lessons continue. I still go and spend two hours a week with Nikos and I am now translating an English novel from Greek back into English as a way of learning sentence construction and vocabulary. This involves much use of the dictionary and guesswork. The new Mayor has arranged for free language lessons for non-Greek speakers and 15 of us turned up for the first of these at the primary school last Saturday. We made a varied class of pupils; from fluent Greek speakers wanting to learn to read the language, to absolute beginners. But there was a great sense of everyone helping out everyone else.

My new language skills were put to the test when the rent had to be paid to our landlord via the bank last week. I had it all prepared: *"Then milaw Ellinika polli kala alla thelo na pliroso afta ta lefta ston logariasmo…"* and duly recited this to the patient young lady behind the counter. To which I received the reply: "Perhaps you'd better talk to me in English". We've had this a few times but I now insist on replying: *"Prepi na matheno Ellinika!"* (I must learn Greek). This usually brings a smile and I hope it's because our hosts here approve of an Englishman making the effort and not because I've mispronounced a vital verb!

Being English we have to mention the weather which has been varied. On a few mornings Neil has managed a couple of hours sunbathing in our courtyard while I freeze at the computer inside the house. On other days we have been trapped in the house by rain which leaks in under the kitchen door turning the tiled floors into a skating rink. No boats could come and go for a week recently and the vegetables in the shops looked very tired as no fresh supplies came in. Thunderstorms are frequent, quick and dramatic and the wind has been shaking the last of the oranges from the tree. We hear them hit the ground with a thud or a splat. Neil is due to make more marmalade this week. We have been baking bread and experimenting with our cooking skills.

Creatively speaking I have been working on a new novel, aware that I only have three months left to finish something before the summer season of seven day working starts up. Neil has been photographing when weather permits and I have been painting a little.

Pipe and Slippers – the kittens/cats continue to expand and we are now a little concerned that Slippers may be with 'Slipperettes' and that we may have a few pairs of slippers before long. She has a boyfriend now, a white and ginger thing of dubious lineage who courted her without her father's permission and spends happy hours making a dreadful noise in the back courtyard. Pipe is a bit put out by this (being a tomboy she doesn't approve of boyfriends and sissy stuff like that) but it's only a matter of time before she too starts dating and then what, Pipettes? We're waiting anxiously for the volunteer vet to arrive in April. When Greek people ask the name of our cats we have to explain carefully why they are called Pipe and Slippers as, in Greek slang the words translate roughly into some naughty words one of which is 'spank' and the other I can't write here. We didn't know this when we named them, honest.

And the end of the month left with a bang though not as serious as the storm at the start of January. We had a thunderstorm for an hour and February was brought in the next day with hailstones the size of marbles. We get it all here.

That will have to do as the January episode. February promises to bring more cold weather, though hopefully some sunny days when we can get in some mountain walks. Blossom is starting to appear on the trees already and the valleys are carpeted with grass and we have some daffodils coming up in our garden. There is more to be written, photographed and painted and much more language to learn.

Happy new year or as we say here Xronia Polla.

Dear Diva
Saturday 22nd Feb 2003 already!

Where's the time going?

All I've managed to do so far this winter is finish the first draft of a novel, knock off a quick play and get half way through a screenplay. That's probably enough.

What news from England? We've seen pictures of Brighton's collapsible West Pier (or as the old sign, missing two vital letters, used to read: Wet Pie,) and we have heard about the fire on the Palace Pier. Some sort of revenge attack from the old school who are trying to save the Wet Pie perhaps?

Other news from the island: Well, from Greece. Have you seen the state of our weather on English news? Northern Greece is under several feet of snow and the 'emergency areas' have been declared as far south as the Cyclades. Including Paros/Antiparos where we were first thinking of staying. It has been the worst winter for X number of years apparently. Down here it has been wet and is now cold, though the sun is out today. Everyone on Symi is moaning about how this is the worst winter ever. I hate the way that some of the English here do nothing but moan! Yes it's been cold but what's wrong with putting another jumper on and getting on with it? Although we're on a tight budget and getting tighter by the day we do go out occasionally and have had a few long lunches, like 11 hours long.

I can now fit into some jeans not worn since Gran Canaria (the 'thin' visit) and the belt is done up another notch. I have four hours of Greek lessons a week and Neil has two. And, as soon as we are more certain of non-rainy days, we will be off for long hikes. Pipe and Slippers are doing well, though Slippers (Slappers as she is now called locally due to her continuous state of hormonal overdrive,) is now definitely up the duff and so we'll soon have a whole rack of little footwear to either drown or rear.

How to spend a week in February:

Monday:

Planned walk to St. Vassillios bay does not happen on account of strong wind and cloud, it's a day for keeping warm indoors. There's your first joke of the week – it's colder inside than it is out. Call friends to invite them up for coffee. Maybe it's our position up the mountain but friends launch counter-invite and we are persuaded down to Pitini for lunch. Collect wine and beers en route please – it's going to be that sort of lunch. Arrive at friends' house in power cut, light candle and huddle around it. Forget about half cooked spaghetti and tuck into salads, bread, wine and Greek practice. Electrician called, arrives, declines invite to booze up and fixes mains switch. Seven pm; lunch finishes and a quick drink in the Glaros bar on the way home. On way to bar get offered day's work for tomorrow and regret having that last glass of Retsina, so have a bottle or two of beer instead.

Tuesday:

Spend day in empty old house sanding woodwork and getting to know every inch of the huge, internal, double doors with intricate frames and mouldings. How many layers of paint? Probably getting lead poisoning if not hypothermia. Wander home later with aching arms and covered in dust, looking like a real worker. Pass Glaros bar, resist temptation for drink and to show off my workman's outfit, see – not a tourist anymore!

Wednesday:

Sun's back! Neil in the courtyard in shorts, a sunbathing day. Work on screenplay idea. Computer is in the house, may as well be in the fridge. Type sentence: 'Wr oykk nacj do diiii yje idnald.' Unfreeze fingers and have another go: 'We pan around to see the island…' Going to be a long day. Make most of new (second hand) CD machine and listen to music. 80% of radio stations Turkish, but play some borrowed CDs. What will happen when they are returned? Snatch a couple of hours in the sun before it disappears at four. Both spend evening reading screenplay out loud. Will spend tomorrow cutting it!

Thursday:

Dash to harbour. News just in: *we have mail*. Turns out to be a German shoe catalogue; mother has been putting me on mailing lists again. Trip to bank and gird loins for monthly phone call to landlady in Rhodes: we are paying rent today. First half of Greek/English conversation goes according to script. Then landlady forgets script and goes off on tangent, she improvises in Greek at

17

breakneck speed. Try a bit of Grenglish but it doesn't work. Thrust phone at passing Greek friend with look of desperation and miracle occurs. Landlady finally has compatible bank account. Paying rent no longer involves boat trip to Rhodes and can be done at bank without too much pain. Go to bank and use 'bank script'. It works! (With the help of Greek friend in back ground nodding encouragingly and giving useful tips like 'accusative', 'past conditional', 'epsilon'). Yippee, rent paid for two months in advance and no blood spilled. Spend afternoon in courtyard and in evening attend the Sooty festival. Nothing to do with shoving your hand in a glove puppet. 'Soot Thursday' (very loose translation), the last chance to eat meat before Lent sets in. Free souvlakies and wine. And us being vegetarians! Whole village turns out into square, kids in fancy dress – the best we've ever seen – and older youths in sillier costumes. Some daft English like me turn up in army jacket (only winter jacket that would fit in luggage) and green jeans. Much amusement caused, am I to enter the competition as a soldier? Ha blooming ha, another wine please… Neil dances with the women in what was traditionally, until then, a women only dance and I slur/talk to my Greek tutor in perfect Greek.

Well I think so.

Friday

Behold, more sun and a rise in temperature. Neil only wears jock strap now. Courtyard not overlooked, well only by the congregation of our church 50 yards away. But no service today. Washing everything and getting winter damp out of clothes. Reading book (and shoe catalogue) sent by mother and translating reading book for Greek lesson in evening. Said lesson goes well, Nikos very pleased with my progress now I am sober again. An evening spent in the company of James Bond on TV, drinking hot chocolate and curling up with the cats.

Saturday.

You get some sort of weather here every day. Cloud mainly at this time of year. Cloud with rain in it. Municipal Greek lesson today, down at primary school with the other English from 11 to one. The cast of our own version of Eldorado assemble to learn in stunned silence about the conjugation of masculine nouns in the singular and how to handle the stress. (It's a vital piece of grammar that stress.) Emerge two hours later with ponocephaloi thumping away- that's headaches to you - and collapse into a cup of coffee. The walk home helps reactivate the brain. Collect bottle of wine for party in Pedi valley tomorrow on the way and settle down to work on completed first draft of new screenplay. Discover file has been corrupted and all 130 pages lost forever.

Drink bottle of wine.

Sunday

Shouldn't have drunk the bottle of wine. Now have to find an open shop and ponocephalos not much improved.

Dear Diva.

It's Sunday morning again already and while Neil snores merrily away in the west wing I have risen early thanks to church bells and a noisy sheep. Only two days ago, while pegging out washing in glorious sunshine I spied a man in the ruin outside our courtyard doors. I gave the standard Yasou greeting to receive the traditionally Greek reply of 'morning mate!' He left behind a sheep and its lamb. A very noisy sheep at that. The lungs of a basso profundo and the vocal projection to match. It sounds like a rather uneducated stallholder from Ridley Road market on a Saturday morning shouting 'yeah' every ten seconds. Blooming thing must be warming up for an appearance at Glyndebourne! The good news is that it will move on when it has eaten all the wild daisies and grass that are currently growing there. In the meantime we have a neighbourly fog horn with no fog. It matches our other neighbours, the chickens that sit in trees and panic about nothing all day, the cockerel that has no idea of time and the family of goats. Goats are much better behaved on the whole and provide no community problems apart from a faint whiff which you can only smell when on the roof. Oh, and our local donkey has just stuck its head in through the courtyard gates; just checking that everything's o.k., seeing if there's anything edible in here. No? He's off.

Well that's how Sunday is starting. It promises to become more surreal as we have our carnival parade today down in the harbour. All of Greece, it seems, had theirs yesterday but Symi has it today. Which is just as well as we had about three inches of rain yesterday but today the sky looks more promising. Our local bar, Glaros, that's seagull to you, had its masked ball on Friday night. We didn't go. We had thought about putting on full drag and Venician masks and making an entrance but we'd probably have been the only ones there doing so and we already have a reputation for being eccentric. Glaros bar's idea of a masked ball is to take all the tables and chairs out, turn the volume up another few decibels and turn all the lights out. So there would have been no point in wearing a costume. Hey ho.

The sheep has gone strangely quiet. We weren't expecting that until Easter when the lambs will be slaughtered...strange place this.

Re. Australia. Of course! Or as we say here in Greece, vavaios! If you can swing us some gigs with no huge expense to poverty struck me then count me in. If anything comes up between the months of November and March/April then I'm up for it. We're still not sure what our follow on plans will be come the end of our year here. At the moment we're keen on the idea of spending another year here if we can save enough money during the season to do it. I couldn't face the idea of returning to a nine to five rat race life, nor the idea of sharing our house with lodgers to make ends meet again. Sadly we'd have to do both if we came back to the UK full time, at least until a job produced enough to make the lodgers redundant. Unless we sold the house and rented, in which case we could go and do whatever we wanted. Still debating ideas and will wait to see what the summer holds. The winter has been great but the summer (with 70 hours a week for £2 an hour in temperatures over 100 degrees) may change our minds. As far as I know we can keep this house for another year or two and the rent can, in theory, be paid for by the income from the lodgers back in our English house. We have set a date at the end of August to decide what to do next. However we are keen on the idea of returning to the UK for Christmas this year. We shall see.

Oh, the sheep has woken up again, just heard a G below middle C.

So, what exactly have I been doing these last six months which seem to have flown by? Well, once settled into the house, once the post season parties finished - not that they ever have, there's always some social event going on - and once I'd got my head into gear, I've: Finished off 'You Wish' and sent the first draft off to the agent. Still waiting to hear feedback. Finished off first draft of another novel. Neil's now reading it for obvious errors etc. then one more read through and off to the agent. I knocked off a quick idea for a play and sent it to Carl in case he liked it - haven't heard from him as yet. So you never know by the end of the summer the agent may have sold a book, I may have sold the screen play and all could be right with the world. Doubt it though. Have also tinkered with the plot for an opera, started another novel which then became the screenplay, painted a few rocks and learned a bit more Greek. Oh, and lost two stone. Read hundreds of books, walked, looked after a dog, baked bread, launched a boat, and written a letter to the mayor.

So I've not been idle.

Now don't forget to organise yourself to come and visit. We're not yet suffering from island fever but we do miss certain people from home and it would be lovely to entertain you here if you can make it. Neil should be starting work again in April and I'm still waiting to hear about a job. Failing that I'll be sweating in a silver shop or tripping over chairs in a taverna somewhere.

Neil is now up so there goes my quiet morning. He's already started sneezing and yapping and worrying the sheep.

PS: Help! In dire need of suitable music to play on new/old CD/tape machine. Any chance you could do me some selections from shows on a tape or CD and post off? Only if not a huge problem or expense. We only have Elaine Paige's Anything Goes and it's all gone!

March 2003

Blimey, where to start? Obviously the most memorable day was the birthday, the big 4 0 birthday. It started with the sunrise, which is always a good sign and an early start as Neil and I were walking (with a friend) to the other end of the island. First shock of the day was the gift of a bright pink mosquito net for the mousandra, (sleeping platform). And we are talking Barbie doll, florescent, get those shutters drawn and put your sunglasses on, pink!

The walk was only four hours, up the mountain and across the island hitching a ride for about a mile in a bright pink tipper truck on its way to the dump. (See a pink theme emerging here?) We covered about 12 miles and made it to the monastery of Panormitis by midday, in fact the bell chimed as we arrived at the steps. The church was opened for us and the rather excitable café owner managed to rustle up some coffees to go with the lunch we had carried. Trouble with Panormitis is that it is at the end of the island and once you've walked down to it you have to walk back up. No mobile reception to call for a lift and no cars on the road (apart from the pink truck, long since gone home.)

We did get a lift back in the end. After spending an hour drinking wine with some of the men who live and work down there one of them drove us back to Horio. Well, very nearly drove us over cliffs, into fields and on coming traffic but we made it. Evening was spent with a few friends at a restaurant, open fire, home cooking and good company.

The official open-house party was held on the following Saturday when about 30 people, Greek and English, invaded the courtyard, danced in the salon and generally had a good old noisy time. The local lads came and danced under the orange tree and Neil donned his famous spray on shorts and the bright pink mosquito net and danced in the courtyard. Actually he was very charitable and managed a certain amount of lap dancing with the ex-pat matrons who, one suspects, have not had such a young man anywhere near their laps for a while. Luckily no one needed to be airlifted off the island and no major resuscitations were necessary.

We're actually into April now and things are starting to hot up. Both the weather and the schedule. Neil's boss is back and he's down in the village getting ready the Windmill restaurant which will open at Easter. (Greek Easter being a week after your Easter.) There has been much speculation about the number of tourists we can expect this year due to 'the war' and so on. News on local Rhodes Radio is that several Turkish resorts will suffer but as Greece is not involved we can expect to pick up some of the trade. Talking to some of the reps gives a mixed picture. Crete is doing well, one company has started on Symi and there are now tourists around. (17 this week!) Some companies have few bookings while others don't seem effected. I was put forward for a rep/host job with a holiday company but they have no bookings at their villa until the end of June so I have accepted another job. Mother will love this: I am going to be managing the one and only health food café on the island. The prospective new owners asked me if I would run the place keeping it relatively unchanged this season. So, when it's ready (May sometime) I will be into a routine of eight to four or six, with salads, chick-peas and assorted nuts coming out of my ears. But I am negotiating a day off a week (unheard of!), my 'IKA' paid (national insurance so I can get winter dole money in two years' time) and a management bonus/incentive scheme. Other than that the pay is pretty basic, but if targets are met I'll get *paid* for having a day off. (Even more unheard of.) Neil will be working from five to the early hours again and we'll pass on the steps at around six pm. Or I may see him at the café, or if I go to eat at the Windmill and occasionally (day off) we'll be in the same house at the same time, which will be a bonus.

The other news, literally breaking as I speak, is that Slippers is now a mother and we are grandparents. She's up in the kitchen mousandra at this moment, with Pipe acting as midwife, screaming 'that ruddy man! All toms are b******s' and 'I want more drugs now!' Actually she's being very quiet. We suspected something had happened when I came out of the bedroom and saw the blood... I won't go into details but Slippers was outside looking rather surprised and walking a bit funny. With the help of the animal welfare rep and a mobile phone I searched the house until I discovered a little white thing upstairs behind the spare mattress. Having introduced Slippers to her baby she realised that she couldn't just leave it there and had to do something about it. So she's up there, with Pipe holding her paw and mopping her brow and the kitten is having a feed. There may well be more to come. It's all a bit like General hospital here today and Neil's been really helpful by buggering off to the Kafeneion for a coffee.

The Greek is improving and now that winter seems to be over we are out and about more and are getting a reputation. Luckily it's a good one. Talking (in Greek) to the owner of the Kafeneion recently he let slip that we are known in our part of the village as 'The Boys' (and I'm 40 - read it and weep) and also as people who are trying very hard to learn a difficult language. He told me that some people who have lived here for many years have never bothered and our efforts are noted and appreciated. That was nice, as was the free beer to celebrate. Actually it is becoming difficult to pay for things. It's to do with a) being here all winter and surviving, b) trying to speak Greek and giving people a good laugh with our accents and c) the fact that we will return with friends and tourists etc. but many of the café/restaurant owners have been throwing freebies at us. For example yesterday was almost written off because the previous evening we had eaten out. Our meal and wine came to only 10 euros, but have another half a carafe on the house and have an ouzo to finish off (triple measure). Have you tried our local moonshine, don't like it? Have another ouzo then to take the taste away. No it's on the house, no you can't pay but have another one for the steps... You speak Greek very well have an ouzo. But it's two in the morning! So? Just one more for the steps, there are a lot of steps so you'd better have another. And now I know why the alleyways of the village are built so narrow. It is to keep you upright as you bounce from one side to the other while trying to climb steps that won't stay still.

So yesterday was officially our last hangover day, time to knuckle down to work. And sadly, readers, that means that there will be less time to write and send these waffling emails. But we will when we can. One of the bonuses of my new job, when it starts, will be the use of the café's internet connection, when/if it's installed so that may help. So, we will be in touch again, just can't say when. Must go now. Pipe is rushing around with hot water and towels, Slippers is screaming for an epidural and Milo (the local ginger Tom and suspected father) is up on the roof smoking a cigar and getting drunk. What a good idea!

April 2003

A quick word about job hunting on 'The Rock' as some people call Symi: Start in October and mention that you will be looking for a job the following year. Talk to potential employers in November, wait throughout December, Jan and Feb. Discuss and negotiate during March but don't assume all is as it seems. Just you wait for April! Below is a list of jobs recently offered, considered or discussed. Which one do you think would best suit a 40 year old, vegetarian writer?

- ✓ Managing a health food café (for existing owners)
- ✓ Running a villa for singles holidays.
- ✓ Waiting tables etc. for 16 hours a day on the other side of the harbour.
- ✓ Waiting tables at a beach taverna. (1)
- ✓ Working on a variety of building sites.
- ✓ Managing a health food café (for *new* owners)
- ✓ Waiting tables at a beach taverna (2)
- ✓ Selling leather goods in a shop in the harbour
- ✓ Barman at an internet café/bar
- ✓ Doing odd jobs and fixing people's computer problems

Well suddenly these are the choices and with funds rapidly running low a decision is needed today (30th April). And it's not just a question of which pays the most money - answer: none pay very much. By the time this email is sent I should have decided and I'll give the answer at the bottom of the page. But in the meantime I have been doing the last one thing on the list. Yesterday we helped a couple move house and then went on to fix some PC problem for another couple before doing half an hour's dictation/typing work for someone else. In the meantime Neil painted a floor pink, (but that was what they wanted).

Last night a group of us sat outside the kafeneion for a couple of hours in T shirts (for the first time since last year) and congratulated ourselves on surviving the winter. Tourists are starting to return and the temperature is really heating up. Businesses are starting to reopen (hence the job possibilities) and there is an alarming amount of white thigh and burnt nose to be seen.

Easter has just happened and what an experience that was. On Easter Sunday we went to the church on the Castro and stood watching the spectacle. At about 10 to midnight the lights in the church went off and the priest lit the candle from which everyone lit their own. He came outside a little later and silence fell across the small courtyard. Behind him a very frail lady grasped a bell pull. Our friends who have been living here for some years whispered 'get ready', or similar, as the priest said the words 'Christos anesti' (Christ has risen). The tiny lady on the bell yanked like a thing possessed, the mountain exploded under several tonnes of dynamite, fireworks lit up the sky, red flares fell onto the roofs of houses and the ground shook as if an earthquake had hit.

From the Castro we could look across the valley to our parish church and 50 feet in front of it, our house. The church was apparently on fire and we could see lumps of mountain being blasted into the air before crashing to the ground somewhere in the vicinity of our salon roof. 'It is just like being in the war again' various people reflected as if they'd been there. Kids threw bangers with a variety of techniques that they have been practising for the last six weeks, landing them in the courtyard, under your feet, over the wall, you name it. Others let off rockets from unstable beer bottles balancing on the wall where they were in danger of falling at the critical moment and sending the firework directly into the crowd/church/your face. Our candles were lit from our neighbour's flames and there was a certain amount of 'ooh', 'ahh', 'that was a close one', 'there goes my roof,' 'what?' as the bombing and fireworks continued for a good fifteen minutes. Just as we left the Castro in procession someone let off four dynamite bombs in a row right beside us and we were more or less shaken down the hill and back into the village.

But Easter is about more than just the sound of exploding mountains and gunpowder. It comes at the end of Lent (as you all know) and Lent is observed here more strictly than I remember it being in England. Except by my father who always gave up something for Lent, or at least for the first forty minutes of it. For 40 days some people have eaten only pulses and vegetables and for the home stretch leading up to Paska (Easter) an even stricter fast is observed. So what is the first thing eaten when the fast is off? Soup made from the entrails and offal of the goat/sheep which will be eaten in its entirety the next day. Just what you crave after 40 days of abstinence. Needless to say we didn't. We had home made herb soup and olive bread, cheese pies and red eggs instead. The same as the traditional break-fast meal but without the insides of the animals. Having spent a week in April assisting the vet in cat hysterectomies and castrations the last thing on my mind was offal.

That's another new experience for April: 'Just hold this for me would you', says Martin (the Animal Welfare Vet on his annual visit to treat/spade and see to the stray animals). 'Certainly Martin', I reply taking careful hold of a clamp, 'what is it?' 'A fallopian tube...' I shan't go on. Needless to say I have discovered that I am not squeamish and can now assist in keyhole surgery on cats. Have to say though, watching a tom getting 'done' does make one cross one's legs and cough.

Anyway - back to Easter: Monday night we burnt Judas in the town square, set off more bangers and fireworks and joined in the party atmosphere. Monday we had a traditional English Easter Monday bank holiday by dressing up as characters from Shrek and having a BBQ. As you do. I made a very fetching Robin Hood and Neil was a knockout as the big pink dragon - remember the mosquito net? Also doubles as a costume.

Neil's brother has paid us a visit, our first official visitor since arriving here and we managed one long walk during the week. (The weather was then a bit up and down.)

Two days later:

Job sorted. Previously you were told it would be the health food café, the perfect place for a vegetarian, but the deal between old and new owners has fallen through and if it does open, it won't be until later in the season. Can't wait around that long now that we that we have a new kitten to feed. (By the way 'bootsaki' is doing fine, or 'little dick' as it's currently called.) I am now working eight hours a day (more with overtime as and when needed), for a basic wage + commission and national insurance etc. selling things made from dead cows. Actually it's very well made hand crafted leather jackets and that's not just me doing my 'hractice' (the Greek word for drawing in a crowd of people by talking loudly, making jokes and selling your soul.) The goods are quality and the employer good. I did four hours training and he paid me for the whole day plus some commission on a big sale that he made because I got talking to the customers first. Yesterday, seeing the state of my boots, he gave me a pair of sandals to have, off the shelf, 70 euros, so I think I'll be staying there as long as I can practice my hractice and draw people in. I've never been so bribed into a job before. It also gives me the chance to watch the tourists arrive and go and chat to people. The owner and his wife are Greek and I can practice/learn the language. (As well as French, German, Latin or anything else I can remember to use on the various nationalities who pour into the harbour from Rhodes each day.)

And finally: the sun's back with a vengeance bringing with it the first spiders, mosquitoes and tourists in horribly tight shorts! (The tourists that is, the spiders wear trousers and the mosquitoes go naked.) I'm sure there will be more on all this soon.

A walk on the wild life side
Dear all

A word of advanced warning. Best save and read off line. I feel in a rambling mood.

Just starting on week two of the job which will no doubt be giving Mother nightmares. Me a vegetarian! Now working selling dead cows. Sorry Ma, but needs must. The health food café situation still unchanged, it's like a soap opera, and it's still not open and probably won't be this year. Therefore I'm now committed to selling dead calf and lamb skin to rich and poor tourists alike. But it's a good job. Can't remember if I gave details before but basic wage, National Insurance (and Tax!) paid for me, commission, overtime, free shoes and Greek lessons. All I have to do is stand in the heat for eight hours a day speaking as many different languages as I can remember. (Confusing the French is always fun; telling old ladies from Paris to try on the shoes and then look at their reflection in the ice cream is my favourite so far. Anyone know the French for mirror? Funnily enough 'Mirror' spoken with an 'Alo 'Alo accent seems not to work.)

And the walk to work is great:

Leave home at 8.30 saying goodbye to two cats, one kitten and a puppy. (Neil) Step over fallen oranges outside and machete my way through the overnight cobwebs. Down to the parish square, dodging the dog do, fallen figs and nosey neighbours. Say kalimera to the lizards already basking in the sun and send them scuttling into the ruins in shock. Meet goat which seems to have slipped her moorings and is always drifting about the steps with a full cargo of milk. Explain politely that I have neither the time nor skill to deal with her and that someone will be along shortly. I hope so, or else she will soon need a wheelbarrow to carry her udders. Admonish dogs who left the do as I pass the "320 years ago this house was an embassy" house and wonder when the sign was put up. It looks 200 years old itself so the building could have been an embassy as long ago as... well you work it out. Anyway it's had its day, now it is holiday accommodation. Greet any bleary eyed tourists who may also be pondering the age and relevance of the sign. Pass the lad sweeping up outside Glaros bar and the girl in the chocolate shop. Pass the bakery where Mrs. Baker is now knitting lace, or whatever the verb for lace making is. Kalimera to Rocky the dog with his own sign 'do not pet the dog', which I always feel should be followed by 'or else he might wag his tail at you.' Actually more appropriate is: 'Or he'll have your hand off.'

Through the village to the square and a stop at the peripteron, (kiosk,) to buy a Mother-enraging packet of fags. (Sorry Ma, but at least I'm not eating meat, and I am getting exercise - see below.) The peripteron boys are the ones who christened me Vassilis (because my English name didn't compute in Greek). Quite like having a Greek name - if only it didn't translate as Basil. But it is based on the word for King, so there.

Continue down the steps until the harbour comes into view and see the blue sea, green - now fading - hills, wild flowers (also looking a bit panicked as they know summer is here and the end is nigh for them.) Walk past the senior school - a different kind of animal here, students sitting exams. And wild cats. But the wild cats are in the bins looking for food and a good shag and the students are in class. Or is it the other way round? Anyway, continue down the 'Lazy steps'. Nothing lazy about them. They are steps and sometimes you have to come up them, where's the lazy in that?

Reach harbour and a new form of wildlife hits you - if you're not careful then literally hits you - traffic. First cars since yesterday. And trucks, bikes, mopeds, boats and so on. Noise! Oh my god, adjust into city mode and stroll around the harbour towards dead cow shop. Greet Barbie the dizzy, blonde dog from the winter. Explain for the 500th time that she doesn't belong to me and send her away. Greet assortment of other workers now getting used to seeing me pass. 'Kalimera Katerina... no I don't want a taxi boat. I'm not a tourist. I work here... oh to hell with it! Maybe tomorrow...'

Pass the restaurant with my all time favourite sign: 'Wild goat in oven with potatoes'. Wild? I'd be livid.

Pass the closed health food café and wonder what it would have been like to be inside coking instead of outside under the awning watching the boats come in and haranguing the day trippers. Remember that Thursday is first payday and don't worry about it. Reach work at 8.50 (yes it only takes 20 minutes to do all that) and start my daily arrangements of hand made leather shoes. Wait for the day trippers who descend each day like a swarm of locusts, trying on everything and buying little.

And in the evening - back up the same route, remember it's almost 600 steps. So after daily step aerobics I'm now down to a 33 inch waist and around 11.5

stone. And sometimes I even manage a swim after work and once I have even avoided the kafeneion and not stopped for a beer or five on the way back.

OK. Part two.

(Told you not to read on line.)

It's now somewhere around May 26th. Eurovision has happened (apparently) and Neil has started work. Not in the much predicted Windmill where he worked at the end of last season. It's still not open and as we are two lodgers short back in the UK house, (gulp, panic, I feel a house sale coming on) needs had to and the Devil drove... My boss knew of Neil's plight in waiting for his job and told him that his brother needed someone in one of his shops. 'You would be part of the family,' he said. Which was nice as we've christened the two brothers The Kennedy Bros. due to their empire on the island. So Neil took the job working in a tourist shop three doors away from me. He sells sponges, shirts etc. from 8 - 4 so we get the evenings together although we start and finish at slightly different times. This still gives him time to work on his photo greetings cards and to even work some evening hours if he wants to.

So now we are a two income household and together bring in about £700 a month for doing 8 hours a day, 7 days a week until October. Enough to pay the rent here, save the rent and some spending for the winter and buy salads. It'll do. And we get to wave at each other, or say hello as I pass by to the bins. The best bit though is that he also gets his national insurance paid (we're both in the process of doing our completely unnecessary 'Green Card'/work permit application at the police station.) But it does mean that we will be completely above board and next year, after another season of the same, we will be entitled to winter unemployment money which will easily cover our winter rent here. So assuming we continue in the same vein and don't jack this in and go back to England before then we will be much better off next winter. But this one could be a problem and we may consider selling up, returning to work there for a few months, or working here on the building sites if we can get jobs. Who knows? We will make up our minds at the end of August - one year after setting off.

And finally for this month: Back to the wildlife. Little Kitten is growing, still looks ugly but it'll improve with age. Pipe's still missing a patch of fur from her hysterectomy and we rather fear Slippers has been out courting again. Milo - the Ginger Tom from the neighbourhood - comes and sings to her under the bedroom window most nights which is a real pain in the ears. But that's animals for you. The orange tree has lost some leaves and looks like it might be ill but the roses have flourished and the bougainvillea is starting to flower. The vine has collapsed on the back steps and needs a crutch (next week's job) but at least neither of us has collapsed on the steps yet. Got that planned for August when it gets really hot!

June 3rd - ish.
Possibly it's next month, maybe it's still yesterday. Who knows?

Dear Diva

Slow response to emails these days due to hectic leather flogging schedule and other stuff. Got your mail re Tristan at Glyndebourne, life's too short to sit through Wagner I always feel. Wait till it comes out on video and then you can fast forward through the dull bits and go straight to the credits.

What's involved with 'The trick piccolo'? And which October are you thinking of, this year or next? I'm 'contracted' to work now up until the end of October (this year) without a day off so won't be able to get back until November at the earliest, even if we can afford the fare. Which is doubtful at the moment, with 2 lodgers down at the Rat-House and a meagre income here. But, assuming it's next year, and that it's vaguely interesting and carries with it a ridiculous fee then of course I would be interested in writing the score. Ditto anything which may arise in Australia - or any other colony - during the months of November to March. As I may have said we are going to decide what we're doing towards the end of August, when we would have done our full year. Currently though we are saving for another winter here. We may have to come back to look at the house and maybe work to top up the coffers - or cough up the toppers, pop up the poffers or top up the poppers - but, unless I can find something very well paid for a few months it won't actually be worth the air fare. Then there's the THREE cats to consider. Jack is growing daily and not as ugly as he was, or as she was - still not sure. We can have them looked after if we do go away, or let them fend for themselves so that's not a huge problem.

Anyway - long story short - too late! - we're still not sure what's happening after October 31st, but we're quite keen to stay another winter so I can finish my screenplay and write another book for the agent not to sell. Will keep you posted.

The latest timetable at Villa Skillaki runs like this: Neil gets up at 6.am which means I'm also woken up as he's not a quiet thing in the morning. He goes off to work at 7.30 and I follow at 8.30 (5.30 on a Sunday). Work through 'till 5 and then get my gymnastiki (exercise to you) walking up the mountain, usually stopping for a few beers in the village for anything up to two hours. Back home for housework and sketching, writing or just sleeping. Neil goes from the shop he works in to the Windmill at 4.pm and works through until 11. He'll be doing this until they find someone else or he falls asleep on the job. He is taking Wed and Sun. nights off, apparently. So if we do have any visitors then they will have to fend for themselves until the late afternoon.

We're both fine though. We say good morning and goodnight and occasionally get to chat. We have the six months of winter to look forward to and those long dark evenings in jumpers and hats, watching TV, drinking wine and eating chocolate seem so far away already. Haven't seen TV since March, haven't missed it and can't get drunk now. It was over 30 in the harbour today and as I'm on my feet for 8 hours talking various languages (badly) and not eating until the evening, a hangover is the last thing I need. It's good for me though and we're loving it. Apart from you two and a few other choice people we don't yet miss anything from home.

And thus there's very little news these days apart from the work routine, improving Greek language (Neil now knows nearly all the swearwords and I can decline an active verb. A simple 'no thank you' usually does the trick.)

So, send me more news about Magic Oboe and anything else of interest and I'll let you know as soon as the agent sells a book so that we can all retire! Ha.

JULY 2002

What do the following have in common?:

- The peeling of church bells.
- A donkey.
- A semi-famous pop star.
- A jazz trombonist.
- Chickens.
- The wind.
- A boat.

Apart from making noises that is. Well, they can all currently be heard from our roof.

Tonight (July 25th) marks the opening of the Symi Arts Festival proper. And for the occasion a semi-famous donkey is playing jazz trombone with a pop star, on a boat, in the wind, backed by chickens and bells. Well, not quite in that order. But in this lovely disordered place nothing would surprise. The pop star (in Greece) will be opening the festival down in the harbour tonight and the warm-up can be heard from our roof, carried on the wind as I sit and watch the evening boats come in to shelter from the Meltemi. Meanwhile the goats accompany the church bells in their usual fashion and someone nearby the house is practicing his or her trombone. Sounds like they are rehearsing in the church but that could be a trick of the wind.

Meanwhile: For those of you who thought we'd forgotten about you, we hadn't. There was no column in June due to the work routine and you're only getting this one – if I even get around to sending it – because I managed to get home, write it and then get to our friend's internet connection without getting called to the bar on the way back. That's a Kafeneion type bar not the legal profession calling type bar.

It is Saturday today and since last Saturday evening I have worked for 69 hours. Usually it involves an early morning - which, for me therefore demands an early night in advance – and so, by the time I get home, tidy the house, feed the cats etc. it's time for bed. Hence the lack of emails. (For 'I' read 'we' as Neil does that same sort of hours, maybe 7 a week less – work shy our Neil!)

And as if to prove the point it is now August 1st and I still haven't finished this nor sent it. Promise to try harder and send tomorrow. Everything here happens tomorrow of course.

Today, being the 1st of a month, gives us a chance to wish people a Kalimera (good day) followed by a Kalo Mina, (good month). All well and good. But, on the way home tonight Neil got a bit carried away with his fluency and wished Petros - one of the lads who run our local supermarket - a Kalo mooni. (Due to censorship I can't tell you what a mooni is but it rhymes with hunt.) Needless to say we left the 'supermarket' in uproar and - luckily - fits of laughing.

Oh dear. It's now August 2nd and 6.15 a.m. and I really must just say goodbye before getting ready to deal with the day trippers again. Another hot day in the harbour fending off the usual questions from the tourists: "Do you live here then?" *No, I commute from Barnes on the 6.45 express.* "What brought you to this island?" *I took the bus from Rhodes.* "Oh, is there I bus? We had to come on a boat. Maureen! He says there's a bus...." "What's it like in winter?" *Cold and wet, are you buying anything? No, then Kalo mooni.*

And so on.

September 1st

The anniversary of our leaving England passed on August 28th and we spent the day in the usual manner: working, washing, sleeping. We did sit in the courtyard and list the most memorable things from the past 12 months however:

Booking ferry tickets from Paros down to Rhodes. The ticket stating 11.59 Thursday night. I thought 11.59 was a little too precise a time for a Greek ferry - well actually I thought Thursday was a bit over confident. No surprise then that, just as we settle our six heavy pieces of luggage around us and half order an ouzo our boat comes in at 10.50 and a mad un-ordering of ouzo and dragging of luggage ensues. But we did make it to the ferry.

During the journey we saw the sun rise over Kalymnos on Neil's birthday and I witnessed a group of mourners greet a coffin off the boat on the same island. There's something deep and meaningful there about circles of life but you'll have to ponder it yourselves.

Moving into Villa Skillaki and carrying everything up by hand. We left England with two rucksacks and a laptop and now will need Pickfords to help us move out of here when and if we do.

Taking in the rescue cats, Pipe – found in a carrier bag hanging from a tree – and Slippers. Watching Pipe help with Slipper's first born, Jack, and then helping the Laskarina vet perform surgery on a variety of cats.

Realising slowly that we have moved not just house but country and lifestyle too. Getting to grips with the fact that we may have decided to make the move permanent and are starting to think about selling the house back home and living in Greece full time.

Spending my 40th birthday walking from one end of the island to the other and racing back in a swerving truck to spend the evening with friends in a taverna around a roaring fire.

Sitting in the courtyard at night, watching the stars, feeling the owls swoop low overhead, listening to the bats, the goats, the cockerels and the breeze in the orange tree and wondering why we didn't do this years ago.

End of year one

YEAR TWO
www.symidream.com

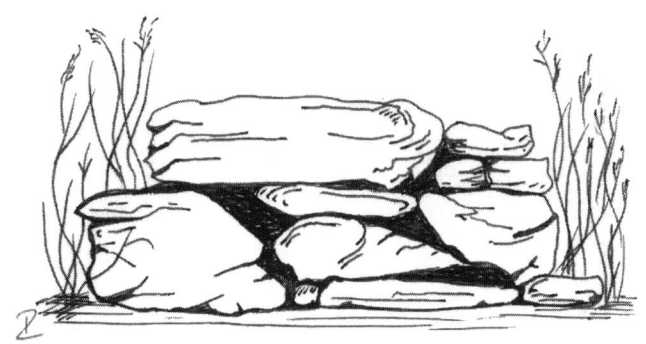

VILLAGE VIEW
& MONTHLY UPDATES

The following pages appeared on our website www.symidream.com from July 2002 onwards. Village View is my monthly column giving my views and thoughts on life on a Greek island (and other trivia). Also included are some of our monthly updates and parts of '24', a collection of short notes describing a different hour of a different day that eventually make up a whole twenty four hours on Symi.

These are all collected here more or less as they appeared on line – mistakes and all! Sometimes they refer to images or other web pages which aren't in this book but I hope this does not spoil the enjoyment.

July 2004

If you have been to Symi, or know it well, you will notice that the picture on this page is not a view of the village Horio, pronounced 'Horio'. It is actually a view of the Pedi valley taken from my roof. And it sums up what this page is all about. It's about how life on Symi is never quite what you think it is. How what you thought would be a straightforward kind of moment, hour, day, week, rest of your life never is. When you live here.

For example: June. I was asked if I would work for a couple of hours a day in one of the village Kafeneion, 'only for a few days.' 'Yes, I would be very happy to help out.' I was actually very flattered to be asked, as a non-Greek, to work in one of the last remaining, traditional Greek environments. 'Just for a few days.' A few days would be fine. I have a draft of a biography to finish and two web sites to get up and running before the end of the month and a couple of hours a day, for a few days, would get me out of the house. 'Just for ten days.' 'Ten? Sure.' 'Or two weeks.' 'O.k.'

Four weeks later and I was still doing my 'few days.' On some days I was doing five hours a day and on one day it was three in the afternoon and another four at night. I have now officially 'finished' the job, but am working tonight, next Saturday, most of September and maybe all of next year. Oh and a couple of days in the winter?

It's this kind of thing that tickles me. (I'm very ticklish.) Like when a tourist with his own boat needs a diver to go down and check something underneath. Now, you can play along at home here: To find a diver where would you go to ask? A) The Port Police. B) The Chandler's. C) The Bakery?

Of course you're right, C, the bakery and why not? It makes sense when you live here. The language is something else we will be discussing at a later date. As these pages ramble on I would like to share with you, from time to time, my own tips for trying to learn Greek.

Lesson one. It is very stressful and the stress is very important. The '*tónos*', little accent that you will see over low case letters, is vital. It tells you where to stress the word so that there is no confusion between, for example, • ••• & • •••; 'when' and 'never'. (Very important to know this if your fiancé has just asked you to marry him.) The word itself, 'tonos' also means tone, touch, trace, shade, force, vigour, a musical tone, interval and Tuna fish.

Lesson two. Things are never quite as simple as they seem. See lesson one.

And that brings us back to where we came in. Now you are probably wondering what all this was about. In a word: a sense of humour. Village View aims to bring you a little quirkiness and maybe a giggle every month so please bookmark and return for more if you can bear it.

August 2004

A trip to Rhodes

Living in the village one soon becomes accustomed to the lack of traffic. That is if we discount the occasional motorbike roaring down a narrow lane and coming at you around a blind corner while attempting the land-speed record. Usually, away from the flat paths, the most one will encounter is a caravan of mules carrying bricks, supplies or luggage up to the more inaccessible parts of Horio. On some occasions one will come across a wedding procession or a group of ladies heading to a christening in smart clothes and dangerously high heels, but in the main the back streets of the village are a quiet, easy place to walk.

Heading down to the harbour one slips into traffic mode and, reaching the bottom of the 'Lazy steps', (you should try walking up them, they are not for the lazy!) one puts on one's 'traffic head.' Suddenly you have cars, trucks and bicycles to contend with and find that you have to look before crossing the road. And then, at certain times, there are the day trippers to contend with, it's a little like being a salmon heading upstream, battling through the oncoming mass of pink flesh, flapping clipboards and cameras.

But all this is as nothing compared to a day in Rhodes. Particularly if, like me, you don't get off the island very much, and let's face it, why would you want to? Well, last week I had to. Neil's children were arriving from Scotland for a two week break and I was detailed to go to the airport to meet them. Quite an adventure, I thought. I could look at shops for one thing and it would be a chance to travel by sea, my favourite mode of transport. The Marina, the 'big boat' as we call it, was due at 9.50 a.m. I never know if the time given by the port police refers to the moment the drawbridge is due to touch down on the quay, the time the bow will first be sighted as it appears around Nimos, or is just a number pulled from a hat. Anyway, after much speculation, discussion and the opening of a book on its arrival time, the Marina finally landed by the clock tower at 12.10 p.m. where the usual pandemonium broke out.

Being a foot passenger with an advantage (I lived in London for twelve years,) I was able to dodge my way aboard without too much injury and found my way to the stern deck to watch the island shrink into the wake as we left. I have always ascertained that the best way to arrive at Symi is by boat. Hang on. It is the *only* way to arrive, unless you are in a helicopter, attached to a parachute or can walk on water. What I mean is, the best way to arrive is on one of the ferries from where you can see the full spectacle of Yialos as you come in, rather than seeing it through the salty windows of the metal tube on stilts they call a hydrofoil. And if you must leave the island then the same is true, you can linger over the sight until the view transforms into hot grey rocks and Symi is taken from you by the heat haze.

And so I watched 'home' slip into the distance with the smug satisfaction of knowing that I would be back in less than 24 hours with the children bouncing up and down in excitement as they got their first view of our island. What does one do on a slow inter island ferry for nearly two hours? I had a cup of almost coffee, watched plastic chairs being dragged about the deck in the wind as if poltergeists were fighting over the best place to sit, and watched the coastline of Turkey pass by. I was first aware that something more spectacular was taking place when I noticed a crowd gathering at the railings to look inward to the boat as opposed to outwards to the sea, the mountains and the potential sightings of dolphins. Obviously something far more interesting than Asia Minor was taking place.

The highlight of the mini-cruise, it seemed, was to be the unveiling of the swimming pool. At one p.m. exactly some plastic netting was dragged back and water started to dribble into a deep hole on the top deck. This brought an air of anticipation to the boat and slowly gasps of surprise could be heard from all quarters. Everyone seemed to be in awe of the sight, as if the Red Sea was parting before their eyes, or Norway was winning the Eurovision song contest but after ten minutes, when the water level had risen only about two centimetres, people started to drift away with looks of betrayal on their faces.

I only mention this so that if you ever travel on the Marina you can turn to your fellow passengers and remark smugly, 'that pool was filled at one o'clock on July 21st 2004 you know,' as if you had been specifically requested to attend the momentous event and thereafter get yourselves invited to dinner to retell the entire spectacular story.

Arriving at Rhodes and the Symi-dweller must quickly adjust to its traffic. Cars, bikes and busses whiz at you from every direction and after crossing the road looking continuously left right and back again, you must head directly to the hospital to have your whiplash checked out. After staring at a traffic light for a few minutes and having worked out what it was, I headed for the Plaza, booked a room and settled in for the afternoon.

I sat by the swimming pool simply because I could and because I hadn't seen a full one for several months and there I had lunch. I was due at the airport at 3 a.m. and so intended a sensible, early night ready for a recklessly early start. As it turned out I got no siesta thanks to someone in the next room watching *The young and the restless* at full volume and Neil's son sending endless texts from Glasgow airport. 'We've got the tickets,' 'we've checked in,' 'we're sitting down now,' 'now we're standing up,' 'we're getting on the plane… in two hours,' 'just been to the loo,' that sort of thing. But he is fourteen and has never flown before so I forgave and decided to see the sights of Rhodes and search for something to buy. What can I get in Rhodes that I can't get in Symi? I went into Marks & Spencer because it was there and caught myself admiring cardigans and socks, a sure sign of imminent old age. After searching other shops in vain for that elusive something I can't live without I returned to the hotel for dinner and then to my room to try another sleep.

No good.

It was one of those 'can't sleep in case I over sleep' attempts where you look at the alarm clock every five minutes and wake yourself up, when on the very cliff edge of sleep, by thinking delightedly 'Oh, I'm falling asleep at last!' I gave up at one in the morning and decided to go to the airport early. My reasoning here was that it would be more entertaining than watching Police Academy Five on the Star channel for the fourth time this year and at least, if I did fall asleep, I would be in the right place.

George in cab 68 drove me to the airport some twenty minutes away in less than ten and by the time we arrived, I'd learned his life story and felt like we'd known each other for years. I always like to entertain the taxi drivers in Rhodes by talking to them in Greek, particularly if they are on the night shift, it must brighten up their working day (or night) I feel; me stuttering away in the present tense and them replying in perfect English. It also takes my mind off death.

At the airport I settled into the upstairs café for what was due to be a two and a half our wait. This posed no problem. One year, returning from Symi on a different set of tickets than we had flown out on, (the topic for a future episode of Village View I am sure) we arrived at the airport twelve hours before the flight was due to leave in order to confirm our seats. With nowhere to leave our bags and not relishing the prospect of dragging our rucksacks around the town for all that time we opted to stay and sit it out. The plane finally took off fourteen hours later by which time Neil had read two novels and I had written a comedy revue entitled 'Club 18 – Hades'. (Which received very good reviews three months later when staged in England, I am pleased to say.)

This night, wandering between the café in departures and the seats in the arrivals hall, I was reminded of what the revue was all about. Package holiday hell; travelling wholesale class from England to Hell and back for the sake of two weeks in the sun. Having lived on Symi for a few years I'd forgotten about the delights of a 2.00 a.m. check in for a flight leaving at 5.00 and, similarly, the delights of arriving at 3.30 a.m. after a four hour flight with knees up to the chest and food in plastic compartments.

In these days of heightened security departing tourists are lined up outside the arrival doors and let in a few at a time. Bags are checked through a security machine before travellers are checked onto their flight and each one is labelled. (Bags, not travellers, although I dare say the day will come. A few years ago I was asked to direct 'Cabaret', the Kander and Ebb musical and my first image for the show was to have the cast arrive carrying suitcases. These would be similarly labelled and then, as the show progressed, be piled up centre stage so that by the end of the night the stage was empty but for a pile of labelled, yet anonymous, suitcases. An image which was supposed to remind the audience that, apart from the fab singing and dancing, the show was set against the rise of the Nazis and has a very dark side to it. Don't know why I'm telling you that, sorry, back to the story.)

I had two teenagers to meet, neither of whom had travelled alone before and I was starting to get nervous in case they had done something teenage-like on the plane. There was one heart stopping moment when the announcer of flights and urgent messages called for a Mister Kallhnghnghs to come immediately to the police station. I didn't hear the announcement again though and reckoned that if it was me they wanted (because one of the children had tried to smoke in the toilets, or take a stroll outside or something,) they would call me again. They didn't and so I hung about at arrivals watching the Reps and wondering what form of dementia or masochism it is that drives people to do that job.

I mean, to spend your summer hanging about airports at all hours in a hot uniform, your hair in an unbecoming ponytail and clutching a clipboard, having to smile and be welcoming to people who think that to arrive drunk and abusive is funny... well I ask you, who would do that? On a few occasions I had new arrivals stagger up to me, trying hard to focus their bleary eyes (either because they'd been travelling since a week last Thursday or because this was their first ever holiday and they had downed two cans of Newcastle Brown Ale on the flight and were not used to it,) and ask:

'Are you Thomas Cook mate?'

To which I replied: 'No, he died in 1892,' or 'you want the lady in the polyester.'

I was even asked, 'are you our First Choice?' but my reply of 'I might be yours but you are certainly not mine,' fell on deaf ears and blank expressions.

When I told someone that I was very sorry but I was not Manos and that I believed he was driving coach fifteen, I may have gone a bit too far as an entire family dragged themselves across to the coach park and were later declared as lost by a very irritated rep. But I said nothing. Shh!

But, three minutes ahead of schedule, the flight from Glasgow landed and twenty minutes later my two charges appeared in the baggage hall, bubbling with enthusiasm and seemingly unperturbed that it was nearly four in the morning. An hour later and two hundred Glaswegians finally saw their luggage appear on the conveyor belt and celebrated with another drink and a Mexican wave as we stepped out into the night.

Where once had queued a fleet of taxis, enough to transport the entire population of Rhodes to their homes, now stood only two and another twenty minute wait ensued. When we did get a cab he had to stop in a neighbouring village to change drivers as he clocked off at 5.00 and apparently his colleague didn't get out of bed until ten past. But we did finally make it back to the Plaza in time for a ninety minute wait for breakfast.

And then, even more finally, we made it to the harbour to catch our onward transport to Symi, on the dreaded hydrofoil. After sitting inside the metal tube for 45 minutes with the air conditioning switched off, and after mopping ourselves and the floor continually with towels, we left Rhodes and headed for home.

Now then, I don't know if you've ever sat in an oven with a fourteen and sixteen year old who have not slept since yesterday morning and who have lived all their lives in the refrigerated climbs of North East Scotland, but to try and enthuse teenagers suffering from sleep deprivation and heat exhaustion at nine in the morning is not easy. I tried to keep them awake by pointing out interesting things – we had sat right at the front so they could get the best, though limited view as we arrived – things such as: 'oh look, a boat.' 'That's a ferry.' 'That's the coast of Turkey.' 'There it is again,' 'No, that's still Turkey.' 'I spy with…' And so on. But, to give them their credit, they didn't once ask 'are we nearly there yet?'

We rounded the headland and Yialos came into view. 'Look,' I cried, itching with primary school teacher like enthusiasm, 'there's Symi, this is where we live! Isn't it…?' But by this time they were snoring merrily away. After a nudge in the ribs one of them opened an eye, squinted out at the majestic view, said 'oh', and promptly fell asleep again.

Dad met us from the tin can on stilts and whisked them by the hand around the harbour to have second breakfast at the restaurant where he works. I followed behind like an unfit Sherpa who only took the job because he needed the money, staggering under a sixteen year old girl's make up bag, and fell into a welcoming cup of strong coffee. Dad had to stay and work but we pressed on, an hour later, to the taxi rank where we waited for half an hour before deciding to walk up. Up the 380 odd steps to the house, at noon, in July, with two teenagers who had not slept properly for a day and a half.

But at least when we got to the village and dived en masse into Yianni's ice cream fridge, there was no traffic.

September 2004

A kapnodoxos has landed in my garden

A strange thing to wake up to; an earthquake.

Well, two actually and apparently there had been several more during the night and the previous day. You have to understand that by 'earthquake' I don't mean the kind of thing that brings buildings tumbling down and Hollywood stars of the late 1970's running to rescue Shelly Winters from a collapsing staircase. Not for us at any rate, thankfully. The rumbles that we get here from time to time are, in the most part, not too serious, though there has been an epicentre or two too close for comfort in the past. It's a strange thing at any time of day, an earthquake. Even just a tremor. At first you think, 'that's a pretty noisy lorry going past.' And then you realise that you are no where near a road capable of taking a lorry and you think, 'plane going low over head.' Or, 'very big ferry pulling into the harbour.' But, again, you are not on the flight path and not near the harbour. And then your insides start to vibrate, and you check that you are not sitting on the washing machine during its final cycle. When everything around you is vibrating, shimmying, trembling, dancing and/or simply moving of its own accord, then you realise what's going on. And usually by then it's over. But it still leaves you feeling uneasy and thankful that you were only on the edge of it and not in the epicentre.

But it's still a strange thing to experience. Stranger still is going out into the garden to find a chimney pot lying flattened under your lemon tree. This is a metal chimney by the way. A steel tube with a pointed hat that makes you wonder if the Tin Man has had one pint of Castrol GTX too many, strayed from the yellow brick road and stripped off. In your garden.

You check the roof to make sure your chimney is in tact, yes it is, and you check on Jim's next door. That one seems to be in place, as do all the others you can see on the surrounding houses. So how did it get there? It clearly landed hard, hence its almost two dimensional appearance, but no one seems to be missing theirs.

Later, in the harbour, I check in with Hugo.

'I found a very strange thing today,' I report. 'Someone else's chimney pot in the garden.'

'Ah,' says Hugo with a knowing nod. 'That'll be your kapnodoxos then.'

Well of course, why didn't I think of that? Before I give in and simply ask what a kapnodoxos is, I split the word and get a rough idea. Kapnos… smoke, kapnizo – I smoke, I'm getting warmer. Ha ha very funny.

'Kapnothoxos,' Hugo continues as I'm clearly not going to get all of the connections. 'Kapno, meaning smoke and thoheio,' (or more precisely: doxeio; where the 'th' is a delta and the x is pronounced somewhere between a ch and a good pre-spit hoik.) 'Doxeio, meaning receptacle, vessel or chamber.'

'Ah yes,' I agree, 'that will be it then.'

He reminded me that we had strong winds the night before and it was probably the wind, rather than the earthquake that landed the smoke-receptacle in the garden.

Mystery solved: a couple of days later and I'm pottering around the house when I hear Jim, next door, talking loudly to a Greek lady about cats. At least he is talking about cats, she is talking about wind. And then she mentions her roof, to which Jim replies that most of them are strays. She comes back with something about the builder's mess and Jim denies all knowledge of poo in her courtyard. I get the impression that someone isn't understanding someone and pop my head out to a) see if I can offer to help and b) have a good laugh.

I join Jim on the roof terrace where our buildings meet and see that he is talking across a couple of houses to our neighbour but three, who greets me with a pleasant wave and a hopeful look.

'I think she's complaining about the cats,' whispers Jim. 'But they're not mine, they're all strays.'

And then it all falls into place, thanks to Hugo, as our neighbour mentions her kapnothohos, (or kapnodoxos depending on how you like to read Grenglish.)

'Ah ha!' I say, delighted that I appear to understand. 'I have a stray chimney pot under my lemon tree, is it yours?'

Our neighbour's face lights up when I hold up the Tin Man's left leg and she is reunited with her smoke-vessel. I take it around to her house which is indeed full of builder's mess and because I'm English, apologise for the chimney's flattened condition. She doesn't mind and we chat about the wind for a while before I am shown the family photo album, the house and the open space where she hopes to have a roof very soon. She lives in Kalymnos and has popped back to oversee the repair work, all her four daughters are married and so, now, is her son and her husband is a policeman on Kalymnos and I speak Greek very well.

'Not really,' I say honestly. 'I am still learning.'

'But you know kapnodoxos!' she applauds me and then says something very fast and technical that I don't catch. Obviously if you know smoke-chamber in Greek you are beyond A Level standard and expected to know every single Greek word and verb conjugation.

But we passed a very pleasant half hour, I got to meet one of our neighbours thanks to a high wind and we managed a conversation about families and chimneys.

Was Jim my father?

'No, I just happen to live next door to him.'

He likes cats doesn't he?

Ah, well...

November 2004

Text and tranquillity

After the madness of last month's Tabloid Rant Shock Horror, (which is not included here because it was all graphics and silliness; basically I had caught sight of an English tabloid newspaper and was outraged at how it treated the reader, i.e. as if I was stupid,) there are only two things I want to discuss with you today. Text messages and tranquillity. We'll get the text thing over with first.

It's only a small thing about miscommunication really and a warning to all you text-lovers; those who like to cram as many words into the 160 character availability per MSG/SMS (message) as possible by the use of abbrs, (abbreviations).

Let me give you an example. The message (a little licence taken but more or less accurate) I received from Amanda one Wednesday read:

Wld U like 2 go wkng + me on sat?

Filling in the missing letters *very* carefully I came up with: Would you like to go walking with me on Saturday? I replied: *Wld luv 2*. And the reply was: *Will txt when kno the plan.*

All well and good. Friday comes and I send the message: *N E plans 4 avrio?* (Tomorrow) And get the reply. *Can U come at 7?* To which I reply: *Will set alarm and wait to hear from you*. Reply: *No, 7 in the evening*. I text back: *Thnk god! C U Avrio.*

Saturday comes and I'm still thinking that it is a bit odd to go walking at seven in the evening as it is starting to get dark around then, but I am dealing with Amanda and maybe she fancies walking to Pedi for supper or something. Later in the morning I get another message: *Can U come at 6.45?* To which I reply: *I will come to the house I suppose?*

Finally, and luckily, the telephone rings rather than pings and there is a voice on the line – a bit old fashioned but there you are. It is Amanda:

'What do you think we are doing this evening?'

'Going walking?'

'No! I was asking you if you would like to work with me, not walk!' (Which is kind of a relief as wkng could be short for a few other things that we shan't discuss here.)

So there you are, what I thought was going to be a pleasant, early morning walk in the warm October sun ended up being as a pleasant couple of hours *wkng* at the Windmill. It's a good job we resorted to speech I suppose otherwise I would have been hanging about at Lemonitisa until all hours while Amanda waited for a waiter at the Windmill.

And so on to the other thing: tranquillity.

The scene: A Saturday lunchtime, Symi, late October. The season is all but over, the sun is out and the air is cooler and clear. I take a break from the desk and saunter down to the village square for an hour's coffee. Our hero sits at the table watching the world go by and notes what he sees:

As the ancient cobbler sips his Saturday afternoon ouzo he signals to the even more ancient Yiannis to come down the steps to his table. It takes Yiannis a good minute to hobble the ten yards, his arms stretched out for balance, his legs jerking as if not quite attached to his hips. Once at the table a short exchange takes place and he is dispatched back up the steps to the kiosk to buy cigarettes for his friend. A journey of about 20 yards and a few more steps. He performs his duty, eventually rejoins the cobbler at the table and is rewarded with five cigarettes.

Young Paniotis bounces past, grinning as always, as if he has just done something very naughty but rewarding and has got away with it. You can tell that he is a local lad; he skips down the steps without looking at his feet, and never trips.

Traditional music plays from the radio inside Lefteris' kafeneion and competes with Giorgio's late lunch cabaret; accordion and tenor, uncertain melody, certain voice. Strangely it is in the same key as Lefteris' radio.

Paniotis ambles back up, blowing bubblegum, moving more slowly now as if his dash down was in vain, or has tired him out. Maybe it is the heat – it is October 23rd and still hot.

Lefteris, our landlord, crosses the square on his moped, toots and nods a smile. He is always on or in some vehicle or other when I see him, and when he sees me I am always in a café.

A new song on the radio, slower and plaintive. Without understanding all of the lyrics I know that the singer is suffering from some relationship problem, part of him is broken and will never be healed. I hope it is only his heart.

It must be work knocking-off time, two paint covered men on a motorbike cross the square. Another stops to buy water from the kiosk, turns his bike and heads back up the lane. The butcher finishes his drink outside the closed Rainbow bar next door, returns his glass to his own shop, closes that and heads home with a bag of something heavy and dripping. A couple of guests leave Giorgio's and the accordion falls silent.

A lone tourist passes, slowly on the steps, fans herself and wanders on up. T shirt and shorts. Same as me.

The vine overhead is turning red, a few leaves fall to the ground like drips of blood as a slight breeze rustles through on its way to somewhere else. The sea to my right and far below looks grey in the shadow of the island but the sky is blue and uncluttered. The rock of Nimos basks and occasionally a few white specks drift lazily across the mirror flat water. Sailing boats.

The ex-postmaster waves a greeting on his way to his house.

A young lad on a moped pulls up at the kiosk and collects cigarettes, and his girlfriend.

Alex joins me and we discuss the end of the season. I look at my watch. An hour has passed. An hour in which nothing, and yet everything has happened.

December 2004

But what do you do in the winter?

This is the second most popular question asked of us by summer visitors to the island. The most popular question is slightly more obvious: "Do you live here then?" And one to which I am still trying to find the most inappropriate reply. "No, I commute from Victoria," perhaps?

So to answer the question, "but what do you do in the winter?" here is a list of things we have done since the summer season finished about six weeks ago.

Entertained my 85 year old godfather for a week's visit. Activities included: Dinner at Giorgio's Taverna, a trip to a couple of mountain monasteries where preparations were underway for the feast of Panormitis, a visit to Panormitis itself, a few days working on the biography I am writing of and for him and various visits to the harbour, friends houses and so on.

Watch the first real storm of the season from the safety of the front room. On some days, watching from Pitini on the south side of the harbour, it is not possible to see the clock tower on the other side because the rain is so heavy. Huge black clouds hang over the mountain, and Turkey and the ground shakes with the thunder that booms and echoes around the valleys. Recently a road was washed into the sea at Pedi. You know when bad weather is expected as the boats get moved out into the harbour away from the sea wall; and you occasionally hear an announcement over the island tannoy suggesting that car owners may wish to move their cars away from he bridge, just in case.

Go water-skiing on the Kali Strata. Well, almost. The rain comes down from the mountains, through the top of the village and gathers momentum and tides as it moves downhill towards Yialos. Sometimes, outside the village Kafenion, the water is so deep and fast that walking the steps is neither advisable nor possible. Any excuse to stay inside and order another beer. "I'm just waiting for winter to be over and then I'll go home..."

Here's another game. Not only does the rain sweep down from the mountains it also sweeps into the kitchen, via the light fitting and into the toaster usually. The game here is to mop up as you go and make your breakfast without being electrocuted. This game has been made slightly less interesting by our landlord fixing the leak for us. Now we play 'empty the well before it overflows'. Baths (yes we have one!) are a regular occurrence in our house, if only to use up the water! (This event will not be illustrated.)

Throw another sofa on the fire. Thanks again to our landlord we now have a comfortable sofa and we are the envy of everyone with traditional Greek furniture. As for the old one? Well it was heading for the skip so Neil chopped it up, sawed it to bits and generally made kindling out of it (with great relish) and now we throw bits of it onto the fire while lounging smugly on the new one. What with the real fire, the soft sofa, the DVD, TV and video it is becoming increasing difficult to leave the living room... and fit into my trousers.

And finally. A few other things done so far: Pop over to Jennifer's to feed the cats while she is away. Dinner with Kobi. Dinner at Giorgio's. Drinks at Lefteris and Rainbow. Shopping. Dinner at Jenine and Ian's house. (You notice a theme recurring here?) Lunch with Jane. An evening or two at Jean's bar. Sunday lunch at Julie's bar. Dinner at home with Nikos, Takis, Esmerelda and Eleni. Symideam meetings and web work. Writing the next novel. More eating and drinking. Learning more Greek, including the words for indigestion and obesity. Making Christmas crackers. Collecting firewood in the mountains. And thinking up a good answer to the questions, "do you live here then?" and "but what do you do in the winter?"

January 2005
Medical stuff and resolutions

December was a strange month - it feels like I've not been out of the house for several weeks when, in fact, I have actually been off the island more frequently than usual. (Twice in one week! That makes five times this past twelve months.)

Due to some medical business I had to pop over to Rhodes, which was handy for shopping as this was just before Christmas. And if you've ever wondered about the medical set up over here and worried that it might be 'not as good as back home' (UK) well don't. Without going into technical and too intimate a set of details let me just say that I had to see a specialist. I decided to go private. So: boat to Rhodes, quick walk up to find the place, a two minute wait and an hour with the specialist (including a go on one of those machines that look through you with the aid of some very modern technology and lots of cold lubrication). I never knew there was so much in there. I had a guided tour of about six of my internals organs, said hello to parts of me that I would never normally see and had a good old chin-wag in English about the state of my kidneys. And other things.

Having been given some rather reassuring results (nothing to worry about - nothing that a few pills won't clear up) I was also given a copy of my scan. I was reminded of one of those Blackpool Pleasure Beach rides where you get snapped just as you go over the edge; I was able to take my photo away with me at the end of the ride.

I got a set of three pictures, (I think I will make them into a triptych) including shots of both kidneys and... well the third one's a secret. But I was quite proud of them and have already shown them to half the village like pregnant mothers do.

I got very good service all for only €60.00 and it wasn't even on special offer. And thanks to IKA (like the NHS in the UK), even my medicine was a bargain. I had to pay full price for one set of tabs, but the other five items came to €17.00 (about £12.00). That's less that £2.50 for a prescription. Now, I ask you, back in the UK would you: get to see a specialist one day after seeing your G.P., have an ultrasound and a good in depth chat about your condition at your leisure, walk away with a souvenir photo-set and pick up thirty days supply of medication all within two hours and for less than fifty quid?

Just to put this great event into perspective: Back in the UK in January I waited 3 months for the same thing, only got 3 minutes with a rather grumpy NHS specialist (couldn't afford private) who didn't explain what he was doing 'down there' and nothing got treated. No photos either.

And so to the New Year resolutions

(The following list is not legally binding:)

I will not make any new year's resolutions - apart from:

1) Give up smoking. (Only possible in Greece if I can get the correct permits from the Prefecture, show my tax number, register with the appropriate department in the town hall, copy my passport six times and distribute copies to every official on the island, visit Athens to fill out a 'Living in Greece and not smoking' application, lodge the application with three Embassies, two police stations, five accountants and a partridge in an olive tree.)

2) Write a village view that has something to do with the village

3) Drink less coffee. (See 1, above for the legal process.)

4) Be more funny

5) Keep taking the tablets

February 2005

Radishes and Rallies

"What news from the village of Chorio in January?" I hear you cry. Ah ha, more goes on in the winter than you may think. We've had some rain and radishes have been spotted in the supermarket. That's it. Bye.

No hold on, there must be something else…

O.k. It's mainly about preparations at the moment. Neil's sorting out his new business and all being well, there should be a new shop open in the village in May. He's going to call it SymiDream so no confusion there. There may be confusion however when visitors to the shop realise that he's not selling the usual tourist stuff (and no sign of a radish) but instead will be concentrating on original photography, writing and music. As well as selling places on symidream courses and events of course. I am putting my mind to symidream talks, courses, events and other things to do during the summer and as previously reported, I have been asked back to the Rainbow, A.K.A. Ouranio Toxo, the bar beside Giorgio's. Yianni has asked me to cover the afternoon shift during the season, while Dimitris (1) is in Crete carrying out his National Service and of course I said yes.

Meanwhile: following the death of Dimitris (2) A.K.A. 'Mister Plastics', who had the household shop opposite the chocolate shop along from Jean's, his son George has been working to change the store into a souvlaki shop. Jean is now away for her holidays and so there are no more late nights at the J&T for the time being. Instead we spend the occasional evening in Glaros where Alex, the previous chef at Helenikon, is currently working before going to Milopetra and where Dimitris (3) goes to recover after building two houses each day. Here we also regularly meet Manolis the refuse-cart and Retsina operative, other ex-pats who come for the new heating system and the local Russian contingent, from time to time.

On occasion it is necessary to go to the harbour, I am averaging once a fortnight at the moment and must remember to take my entry permits. A surprising amount of ducks and geese survived the Christmas season (as did some decorations which are still up) and little has changed down there. Soon we will see chairs and tables outside the tavernas being prepared for summer and large numbers of boxes from the big ferry bringing seasonal stock. There was one private sail-yacht in a couple of weeks ago but other than that little sea-going traffic appears.

And so winter life ticks by slowly. I spend many hours at the computer working on my novels and research for a new guide book while Neil writes his own science fiction novel and works on his photographs. The garden is in need of weeding and we've run out of fire wood. Apart from that, little changes. I did crash a variety of cars, throw myself through a windscreen and took part in a rally through an Alpine forest last Saturday, but that was only on Ian's X-box. I imagine that that will be the highlight of my month; that and the purchase of a couple of radishes, if there are any left after the rush.

March 2005

It's more often off than on – a ramble in the dark

So I'm sitting there one morning, flicking through the TV channels and trying to decide what to watch while I try to decide what to do today. Should I stay in and watch Kalimera Zoi, Kalimera Ellatha, Proino Kafe...? (A little less torturous that watching the U.K.'s Good Morning with doodah and what's it because I still can't yet understand everything being said.) Last week there was a whole hour dedicated to making a huge cheese pie which was quite entertaining, but today it seems to be about a scandal involving a Priest and soft furnishings. I'm sure I have better things to do.

I know, I'll spark up the computer and write something while listening to music, but I'll just put the kettle on first.

Slow fade to black.

Power cut number six of the week takes place.

It's not until the power goes off that you realise how noisy your house is. The new/second hand fridge freezer stops chugging, the TV stops yapping at you and even the video player that you didn't realise made any noise when it wasn't on, winds down. Everything goes quiet and a little bit dark as the shutters and doors are closed against the cold. Peaceful. But what to do? I reminisced.

One night when a power cut happened Neil and I actually found ourselves having to talk to each other, heaven forbid! To avoid the stress of conversation I went up onto the roof to look at the stars. Without the lights from houses and street lamps the view should be spectacular, I thought. But there was heavy cloud cover than night and the view was... well the view was very dark.

As I watched a few candles come on around the village I remembered a time when I was at Jean's bar, not long after we arrived to live here. It was the first November that I had been on Symi and everything was unusual to a previous 'only been here on holiday in the summer' person like me: rain, clouds, cold, no tourists, a new experience.

Even more of an experience was getting home from the bar one night. In a power cut.

We lived at the top of the village that year, just below Agia Triatha, the top church with the big dome and loud bells. (Even louder the morning after a night at Jean's.) Now then, as anyone who has popped in to Jean's for one on the way home will know, there are always two problems. The first is actually bringing yourself to leave the cosy bar, the heating (or air conditioning in the summer) and the chat and the second is getting home. For a start it's always later than you think. The Jean and Tonic is a kind of TARDIS for time. Time passes more quickly inside the bar than it does outside and before you know it it's three in the morning and you've been in there since ten the previous day. And for some reason the houses move as you stumble upwards towards home, they lurch towards you and get in your way. Luckily the guys who built the village back in the old days had the sense to make the alleyways narrow so that, in places, you can touch both sides with the flat of your hands for support.

So, like Samson pushing apart the pillars of the temple, you drag yourself up the lanes, avoiding the step that you don't remember being there yesterday and squint into the blackness as there are now no streetlights - power cut remember? It's a wise idea to keep your feet close to the ground, shuffle and go slow, so as to avoid tripping on the steps, stones and other people sleeping off an evening in Jean's. While doing this you mumble to keep yourself awake; things like 'never again', 'I'm in so much trouble' and 'where the hell am I?'

Until you bump into something. Or rather, someone. Then you curse with shock and your hiccups are cured. But who is it? Grope, grope. Oops, I'm very sorry madam but you are wearing black, you're heavily camouflaged and I'm three parts to the wind. Can I help you find your way? *No thank you, but can I help you young soldier?* (How does she know I'm wearing my tatty old army jacket? I can't even see my feet. Must be an experienced Symi night wanderer.) No thank you, take care. Goodnight.

And blithely on towards your destination. Luckily you won't remember any of this in the morning.

I did get home that night and there were no repercussions from my little bump with a village elder.

So, as I stand on the roof looking through the gloom down to Pedi, I realise that there is a light on. Somewhere just off the road there is a building ablaze with light. It's the power station. So they're o.k. then.

Actually they are working very hard to repair the fuse or whatever blew and before long you start to see things improve. Pedi comes back on line first and then the chain of street lights appear advancing towards you up the road. Half of the village sparkles momentarily and you can hear the power station rev back into life; before groaning into silence and blackness again.

A few minutes later and the same spectacle occurs. This time you hold your breath as your own house lights up, count to ten and decide it's all sorted out now. You can just find your way down the steps, through the garden and into the house.

The heater is back on, the TV has sparked up again and the evening film is just about to start. You get heavily involved with Mel Gibson, as far as the second reel, when suddenly someone plugs in one too many electrical appliances and your world is plunged into darkness again.

Time for bed.

April 2005

A slow walk up a hill and down to the village

This month I wanted to take you on a Sunday morning stroll, but as you weren't here I had to take Neil instead. We missed you but thought of you on our journey. Here is an account of what you missed.

Let's go:

Having encountered a few goats outside the house, (parked up in preparation for Easter, they will be working their way around the village feasting on the grass and weeds before we feast on the goats - not me, I'm vegetarian,) we set off to our first port of call, dumping our bin-bags at the bins by Campos Supermarket. That domestic chore done it's off along the road towards Agia Marina. Not the beach Ag. Marina but the cemetery, just off the main road as you drive up the hill out of Chorio. Stopping for a brief chat with Melanie and Paul, who are working on their new/old house, we wander on and arrive at the turning off towards Ag. Marina admiring the spring flowers.

After some rain the weather has turned unexpectedly warm and sunny recently. Neil has tanned himself, lazing in the sun up on our roof, (while I dug over the garden, planted some new plants and helped Paul angle-grind some oil drums into flower tubs and a compost heap by the way,) and everyone is out making the most of the weather. Which means that the road to Marina is quiet, a few folk drive past and wave - off to a children's party up the mountain, and we wander the newly concreted road towards our destination, the chapel of Zoodhochos Pighi at To Vrysi.

Stop and admire the view back to the village as I read to you from 'Symi, Sentinel of the Greek Archipelago' by I.M. Chatziphotis:

"During the same period (1765 - 1821), a school was flourishing on Symi in the location of Agia Marina where today the graveyard of Chorio can be found. The school was known as the 'Museum of the Symiot Land' and it employed many eminent teachers." Apparently the students were boarders at the school from Monday through to Saturday afternoon - what a good idea.

Outside the graveyard are more spring flowers, daisies I think, and from here there is a wonderful view down to Pedi:

Neil stops to take a few shots with his far superior digital camera as I take a swig of water. It's hot out of the shade and you should always walk with plenty of water, even in March.

We continue our wander up the slight hill towards our destination, stopping only to take photos of the wildlife, goats and sheep mainly though there is a bird of prey circling ominously overhead - but we have water so that's o.k. I think it was a kite (the bird type, not the type with strings and small children attached) but it's been many years since I was a member of the Young Ornithologist's Club so can't be sure.

We are further from the village now and the scenery becomes more lunar as we walk further around the valley. Strange plants surround the road as well as better known ones like sage and oregano…

… and more daisies.

Approaching To Vrysi we think we spy tourists (some have been spotted in Horio recently and there have been some day-boats from Rhodes already,) but it turns out to be a couple of chaps working on the land beside the monastery.

After a quick sit down and some more water it's time to wander back to the village for the afternoon. Passing a tree that appears to be for sale as there is a big 'for sale' sign nailed to it, we head to Ouranio Toxo (that's Rainbow to you) where Yiannis is doing up his toilets, (new doors and floors, - regular visitors will be surprised and delighted to learn) and where we sit for a beer or two before joining friends next door at Lefteris'.

And so the warm afternoon passes slowly, with talk of planting seeds for the garden, photography and tourists (those spotted were actually visitors from Athens). Yiannis, next door, goes off for a couple of hours and we are still there when he returns. Michaelis arrives for his regular coffee and has a chat…

And it is not long before the afternoon starts to cool into the evening. Time to get home, get the boots off and apply moisturiser to a slightly glowing nose. (Glowing from the sun, of course, not the afternoon beer.)

May 2005
Beeraki - a tradition

Just off home for Saturday evening tea but need a few supplies first, so pop into Noufris' supermarket. We try and vary our patronage of the village supermarkets, going to shop at Michaelis, George and Petros' shop one day and Noufris' the next. Noufris often has produce produced on his own farm down at Marathunda so it's nice to get some really fresh eggs and local feta from time to time. What special offers has he got today? Aha! The ritual of Beerakai is on the menu.

If you have never had a Beeraki in a supermarket in Greece you really ought to try it. It's a tradition up here in the village. Here's how it works:

Wander around the supermarket for a browse. (For the uninitiated it's not like a supermarket in the UK – there are no trolleys, no nasty musack and no aisles to be had, not even for ready money.)

Collect a one-handled basket and take it to the other part of the shop, up the lane and around the corner out of sight of the staff and have a rummage for muesli.

Return to 'main' part of shop, via the new vegetable rack and squeeze in – to the shop, not the vegetable rack.

Receive warm, friendly greeting from the owner and accept offer of Beeraki.

Owner squeezes out from behind the counter (where he has more room than the customers on this side of the counter) and vanishes outside for a moment leaving you to make small talk with other locals who are hanging out at the freezer talking about how the wind is cold this evening.

Owner returns with your Beeraki and one each for himself and other guests. Everyone pops their Beeraki and merrily enjoys them while discussing issues of no importance whatsoever. Beeraki's are best enjoyed with an accompanying cigarette across the cheese counter it seems.

After half an hour of the Beeraki ritual you finally get to put your one-handled basket down on the counter and are surprised to notice that you have not added any impulse buys to its contents. (Apart from two Kinder eggs, mosquito spray and some interesting looking biscuits.)

Finish Beeraki and leave your empty Amstel can on the cold meats, as instructed, before wishing assembled company a merry evening and squeezing out into the cool wind with hiccups.

By the way Beeraki is a small beer, sometimes it's ouzaki, or even Whisky-aki, it depends on what mood your host is in.

June 2005

As I say yamas to a Danish friend sitting next door at Lefteris' kafenion I spy old George heading down the path towards me cleaning his ears. He heads up the steps towards the sound of the dumper truck. Maybe he can't hear it clearly enough? I wait to see it pull into the square to turn around but it doesn't. I wonder for a while why not; maybe it has reversed back down the lane. It doesn't matter. Once the noise fades away I am left with only the mechanical hum of the fridge inside the bar and a pigeon in repetitive voice. Its song is at odds with the cacophonous sparrows who argue in the vine above me. The birds sing on in a curious cross rhythm that Bartok would have approved of.

Sevasti appears and donates more iced biscuits to our post Easter goody tin. The tin back home is already overflowing with generous contributions from Katarina and Mrs. Anna our new friend who lives beside the shop.

Three girls come down the steps, arm in arm and chatting furtively. All I can make out from their conspiratorial conversation are boy's names.

I wave hello to Yianni next door and an exchange of shrugs occurs. 'Where is everyone?' It is 3 pm on the first Wednesday change-over day of the season. Everyone is in Rhodes, on a beach or taking a nap. We sit in front of our respective kafeneions and contemplate private nothings. Two visitors walk past, silent and white. I say 'hello,' they say 'yasou.'

George's brother Lefteris stops for an information exchange. He remembers the harbour when there were 200 fishing and sponge boats lined up along the quay. His grandfather left to dive the waters off Libya every April, returning in September. A dangerous summer spent working beneath the sea. And did I know that the first doctor to work from the village pharmacy was English? (Approx 1882) Lefteris has a memory beyond his years.

Two pink tourists trudge up from the Kali Strata. Silence returns as the siesta hours drift by.

Suddenly two lads roar through the square on their motorbikes. Perhaps the siesta hours never sleep after all. But, like bad weather up here in the village, noise never lasts for long. Peace is quickly restored, it returns with a slight breeze and a layer of high white cloud.

Noufris calls in on his way to work at Georgio's Taverna – an unusual hour for him, maybe today he doesn't siesta either. I have been jotting my notes for an hour now, only another half an hour and Yianni will return too; the village square will start to come back to life.

Ah, it's started already. Here comes Jim for an ice tea.

July 2005

It is 1909.

The Kali Strata has been expanded and improved during the last century in order to allow the owners of the grand mansion houses a more majestic thoroughfare between home and harbour. Yialos is the business centre of the island and Chorio is the living area. Workers and merchants, sponge divers, captains, artisans and businessmen alike walk from their work in the harbour to their houses on the Kali Strata or in the village. Sitting at the top of the wide steps, Yiannis waits for his crones. He sees first the tops of tall black hats appearing on the stepped horizon. They climb one step at a time to reveal, as if in stop gap motion, the faces, then the suits, then the entire body of the wealthy owners of the sponge and trading businesses.

The gentlemen pass him by, nodding courteously because Yiannis is of the appropriate status, before heading off deeper into the bustling village. Yannis and his friends meet and then make their slow, end of the working day way towards one of the many village squares to join other friends and colleagues for a coffee, an ouzo and an exchange of views before dinner.

In Alemina square George has just opened a new kafenion. Outside, he arranges the tables and chairs around the mill stone that was brought there from one of the old mills. No one can quite remember exactly when or why it was placed there, but everyone has a theory. And everyone remembers the Koukoumas of the spring just passed. The unmarried girls of the village gathered at the mill stone, sat proudly in their island costumes and sung the Koukoumas song. The girls, Yiannis' eldest daughter among them, drew their rings from the silent water and called a boy's name. Maybe that night they dreamed of a boy with the same name who offered water to quench their thirst after the girls ate the salty festival bread. Maybe some of them would marry that boy and fulfil the ancient tradition of Koukoumas. Maybe Yiannis' daughter will marry soon. He has a house prepared for her dowry. She is, after all, fifteen now.

But village conversation on this autumn night is not generally about festivals, but about business; the diving industry, the trade with Europe and the relationship with the Ottoman rulers. The annual tax had been paid, trade is good, the religion remains unchanged by the Muslim rulers and a new bell tower is being planned for Panormitis monastery. The parish churches in the village are thriving now more than ever, only twenty years previously a new one had been completed and down in Yialos, the church of St. John had been restored.

As the men sit, smoke and discuss they decide that life in the village is good. It is busy, most of the island's 25,000 or so residents live up here. Houses stand painted, the lanes are bustling. The village is alive.

The scent of cakes and breads wafts up from the shops and bakeries nearby, the taverna next door to where Yiannis sits is filling up. A train of donkeys passes, heading home. Evening settles in on a cooling breeze.

Summer is drawing to and end, the sponge fleet has been returning for two weeks now. The Skafandro, (once celebrated as the way forward in diving suits, then later known as 'the tyranny' for the agony it caused) is claiming less lives these days as people start to understand the nature of 'the diver's disease.' The island is prosperous. Yes, life is good.

As darkness falls and time moves on there is some background talk of possible trouble between Turkey and Italy. "But that surely won't affect our island. Besides, it is only speculation."

No one knows what will happen in the future but the men, draining their small coffee cups, all declare that Symi is Symi is Symi and they clink a Yamas to their good fortune.

None of them know, nor expects, that within one generation the population of their island will fall by half and beyond that, by more until only one tenth of the people going about their business in the village tonight are left remaining.

The men return to their houses not knowing that soon their property will be taken from them by a country hundreds of miles away. How could they know that couples, who met in Koukoumas dreams that starry, Turkish night in spring, would have children who would grow up speaking Italian?

Note: *A certain amount of licence has been taken in the above. Koukoumas is still an annual tradition and is held on May 2nd at the church of St. Athanasios in Horio*

August 2005

Two weeks as a writer.

01 – Monday

First of the month today. Tried to find a suitable quote. Couldn't so opened a book at random and found this:

"This new tense called past perfect tense will create no difficulties for you. It is formed with the past tense form of the verb *ego* followed by the same unconjugated verb forms in the present perfect."

Teach yourself Greek, (2000 edition) p 222

Perfect!

02 - Tuesday

This time last year it was July 2nd. Strange how that happens.

03 – Wednesday

Our cat Jack had a very trying day today. Firstly he tried to find a comfortable sleeping spot on the back of the sofa but was thrown out when I went to work. Then he spent the day trying to find shade in the garden beneath the apricot tree. He was sleeping quite happily when I popped back at lunch time, until an apricot fell on his head. Confusion followed and he ran around the village telling all the other cats that the sky had fallen on his head. In the evening he tried his tried and tested 'I'm cute and cuddly so FEED ME NOW!!!' act. It's very trying and even though I tried to ignore it, I gave in. During the night someone tried to break in through the open window's mosquito netting, succeeded and brought several mates in for a party in the kitchen bin. Jack was suspected, arrested and tried.

04 – Thursday

Met Velma Kelly and Roxie Hart at the bar this afternoon. Coerced into one too many Bacardi and cokes and far too many references from Musical theatre. (Check your Kander and Ebb. Or in other words: Chicago.)

05 – Friday

Can't remember what I did today so have made something up:

Went to Pedi in the evening for a meal at Julie's bar. Very pleasant – like being on holiday. Must get out of the village more.

Actually that was a Sunday, but who will ever know.

06 - Saturday

Caught a bit of the "Who wants to hold an Olympic games" game show this morning, otherwise titled: 'The prize is right," "You've been gamed," or "Big bother".

TV reception from the Vigla is intermittent and the signal is occasionally interrupted for a few seconds. Fascinating shots of Princess Anne and Sebastian Coe making heartfelt speeches with occasional appearances from a couple of (other) muppets getting excited about the word 'Yiarbar' on a Turkish version of Sesame Street or the Muppet show or something.

So, in case you missed it, the voting was:

Big bird lost out in the first round.

New York went out during a song about how to cross the road.

Some other place was given the thumbs down by Gonzo and Kermit. I think it was Madrid.

There was a break when only London, Paris and a huge pink monster were left in the dance routine.

But finally the Olympic Games 2012 will be held in.... Yiarbar!

(Much merry making, nodding of latex heads and Animal on the drums.)

07 - Sunday

Neil in Rhodes today for essential shop and business supplies. List includes: Sausages and mustard seeds for Marj from that nice deli, shorts for me from M&S, something for Sam's second birthday and various ointments from the chemist that one doesn't like to ask for on Symi 'cos everyone knows you now.

08 – Monday

"What is essential for you to remember here it that the verb form (of the second verb following) called the subjunctive takes the same verb forms in the future tense preceded by Tha. Notice that the same changes occur in the future and the subjunctive in the following examples."

Teach yourself Greek – again.

09 – Tuesday

A new verb has entered the English language: "To Jean"

A few times now I have overheard people admitting that 'last night I got Jeaned.' And so I offer a simple 'declination' of the verb (with translation) to help those of you who are preparing for a holiday on Symi:

The present (active) tense of the verb is straightforward:

I Jean – I go to Jean's bar for one drink

The rest declines as a standard verb.

The future (simple) tense tends to be said with incredulity, involving much eyebrow raising and question marks:

I shall Jean – As in; 'I will Jean it tonight'

You will Jean – As in; 'Are you sure?'

He/She/It will Jean – As in; 'He's obviously not working tomorrow!'

We will Jean – As in; 'You're coming with me to make sure I have just the one drink.'

You will Jean – See the second person singular

They will Jean – As in; "Probably more than once."

The past tense however, is used under a different set of circumstances and usually makes use of the word 'it', lengthening the verb and making it a kind of passive verb, to have Jeaned it, thus:

I Jeaned it last night, which is why I have a hangover today.

You Jeaned it? What again!

He/She/It Jeaned it, he has a note from his mother and is excused games today.

We Jeaned it last night and lived to tell the tale.

You Jeaned it, but you look like you have slept!

They Jeaned it and had a great time.

Of course you can apply various other tenses too.

Examples:

I am Jeaning it... so leave me alone.

I would have been Jeaned... but I put my foot down with a firm hand and left early, 4.00 a.m.

I shall have been Jeaned... at least three times before I leave.

I was being Jeaned... my friends made me do it!

I was Jeaning it... when I passed out.

I have Jeaned it... once too often.

I had been Jeaning it... the night before and missed my flight.

We will be Jeaning it tomorrow and tomorrow and tomorrow...

Not forgetting the imperative: Jean!

Or the Imperfect: I used to Jean it.

And the Collins Dictionary, 2005 edition, definition?

To Jean (it): *Vb. Sing.* To be having such a good time as not to be able to leave the Jean and Tonic bar until dawn – at least.

See also the Oxford book of quotations: "There is no such thing as one drink at Jean's."

10 – Wednesday

Went to Jean's for one on the way home.

Got Jeaned.

11 – Thursday

Written off

12 – Friday

Have to cover the shop this morning, the bar in the afternoon and the shop again in the evening. Then a few hours on the websites. Only a 16 hour day today. Must get around to some writing.

13 – Saturday

Flicked through several books that no one would have heard of as research for 'Jason'. Then did some background work on the musical score which is the key to the mystery, followed by a quick trip to the museum to check something out. Had a brilliant idea for a new twist in the plot. Stopped off for a coffee in the village, forgot brilliant idea. Went home and watched obscure films from the 1960's and some documentaries about football and Communism. Checked out Play.com for some new DVD that no one else would want to borrow and finally to bed at around two a.m. A good day's writing!

14 – Sunday

Sit down to write the next instalment of Jason and the Sargonauts – finally I can get some writing done!

Can't think of anything to write.

I'm off to Jean's…

September 2005

Sit down, no talking, pay attention. A short history of the island follows. I am using as my reference the new and excellent publication from the town hall titled 'Symi, an unspoiled beauty.' Page 17 breaks the island's history down into 19 bullet points starting with the rather specific statement that 'the history of the Dodecanese islands begins in 4000 B.C.' presumably just after the siesta hour.

The Dodecanese islands, as they are now called, were first inhabited by the Greeks (as they are now called) around 2000 years B.C. at least. Early history is vague because people didn't keep accurate records or if they did they didn't survive. (Neither the records nor the people.) I guess no one back then knew that they were historical and had no idea that I would be writing this so they simply didn't think to write stuff down for me. Even if they did I wouldn't be able to read it as I don't read ancient Mycenean that well.

1500 B.C., around tea time, the Myceneans – that's Greeks to you – popped down from the Peloponnese, rather liked the area and settled on Rhodes and nearby islands. Then, again sometime after lunch in 1000 B.C., the Dorians decided to inhabit the islands. I'm not sure where the Myceneans went, probably popped out for a souvlaki, came back to find themselves overrun with Dorians and skedaddled. During this time Homer wrote, sang or recited his Iliad mentioning that Symi sent three ships to the Trojan War and that the local king was called Nireus. Nireus was later buried under what we now call the Pontikokastro (translation: mouse castle). This circle of rocks can be found at the higher end of the line of windmills above Yialos. A few other theories as to what it is include a) an ancient threshing circle, b) a filed in goat enclosure and c) a pile of rocks.

Anyway, we get to the Classical period of ancient Greek history, 550 – 323 B.C. During this time the islands were split between the Macedonians – from the north – and the Romans, from even further north and to the left a bit. Finally the argument was settled one way or the other and the Romans got their hands on Symi. This was in 164 B.C. and the super efficient Romans managed it all before breakfast. Apparently they hung around for quite some time until, in the 7th century A.D. their empire went its two separate ways and the Byzantine, eastern, part of it got to keep Symi, at least until 1309 when the Knights of Saint John, a charitable organisation took it from them rather uncharitably.

Now then, a brief outline of the Knights of Saint John: started as Christian charity workers, wandered about a bit, came on holiday to Rhodes and liked it (Faliraki was only a tiny fishing port then), saw it as a place to stay and do battle with the Infidels – Turks – across the water while protecting the Crusade route to the Holy Land. They set up their hospital but rather liked battles and stuff so got really military, built fortifications on nearby islands, had a few run ins with the Turks, killed loads of people and generally did both good and bad things for a couple of hundred years before the Turks got fed up with them. They took over Rhodes and the other nearby islands in 1522 and sent the Knights packing. They, the Knights, wandered about a bit again for a while until the King of France decided that he didn't actually need Malta anymore and so he let them have it. Very charitable.

Meanwhile, back on Symi, the Turks under Suleiman the Magnificent, settled in on the island and made themselves quite at home thank you very much. They were to stay for 390 years during which time several major events took place on the island.

In 1765 much to the dismay of local children, the first school was founded up at Aghia Marina. (Sadly for them not the beach of Aghia Marina but the monastery just outside of the village – where the cemetery is now.) The children were undoubtedly even more dismayed to learn that it was a boarding school and even though they could see their houses from the dormitories and probably even smell their dinner cooking, they had to stay at the school from Monday through to Saturday each week. Boo!

Maybe it was some kind of payback for being boarders at a school only a few hundreds yards away from their homes but some of the kids developed a rebellious streak. In 1821, when the Greek revolution started, Symi folk were some of the first to revolt. Bravo!

And in 1830, the Dodecanese were exchanged with the island of Euboia, which was annexed to Greece. Not really a fair swap if you ask me. 'Tell you what Mr. Turkish ruler, you let us have sixteen islands from down south and we'll let you have this one in return. It's bigger, more economical to run and we don't really need it anymore…' In the end something went wrong and Symi stayed Turkish. Great boos and groans from the locals.

But actually it wasn't that bad. The island gained a pharmacy, an English doctor, privileges from the Turks, relative independence and during the 19th century, became even more prosperous. General trade did well as Symi kept its special status as a trading port and sponge diving flourished. Until the introduction of the mechanical Diving Suit, the Skafandros or the 'Tyranny' as the locals came to call it. Progress brought all manner of pros and cons. With the aid of the new suit divers could stay longer under water and harvest more sponges, but no one understood the nature of 'the bends', the diver's disease and death and disability returned with the fleet every autumn.

Despite this the islanders persevered. A reading room (learned library) was established in 1872, the first in the Dodecanese and Symi became generally cosmopolitan and wealthy. An Italian and a French architect were invited over to redesign the houses for the bourgeoisie and the Kali Strata was developed into the grand parade that we now see, with mansion houses on either side.

Even many village houses were given pitched roofs, neo-classical facades and colour.

And then it all went horribly wrong. Turkey had a bust up with Italy and Italy got the Dodecanese in 1912. The population of Symi was then somewhere between 20,000 and 30,000 it depends on which publication you read. Apparently it wasn't just the Myceneans that didn't keep accurate records. (Actually most of the island's records went up in smoke but that comes later.) Between 1912 and 1917 over fifteen thousand people left the island and the population dropped by around half. (That's the population of the island today, around 3,000, leaving the island every year for five years. Where did those 30,000 people live? How did they manage for water and where did all the sewage go? Yuk.) The decline continued through the Second World War and didn't start picking up again until the nineteen seventies. The Italians however, while requisitioning land and property, restricting trade and fishing and generally doing bad by trying to good, did manage to introduce electricity in 1928. Now people could see all the empty homes at night as well as by day.

During the Second World War Symi changed hands almost as frequently as dodgy five euro note. The Italians backed out of the island, the war and just about everything else and the island was no man's land for a while. A mad scramble ensued with both British and German forces realising the potential of Rhodes and Kos, with their airstrips, in the war in the Med. The Germans got here first and took over the island. Later the British snatched it back, the Germans bombarded it with incendiary bombs before invading again and so on until finally, on September 25th 1944 they decided they had had enough, blew up the munitions dump and scarpered. Sadly the ammunition had been dumped under and around the Castro and what the Knight of St. John had put up about 400 years earlier came crashing down on the houses and churches nearby. But at least the island was free.

Kind of. The British 'took care of it' until the surrender of the Dodecanese in 1945 and then they kind of took care of it again while Greece got its act together. Finally the island was handed back to Greece in March 1946 but it wasn't until a year later, 7th March 1947 that the King paid a visit, the flag was raised and finally-finally the island became Greek again for the first time in about 2000 years, just in time for supper.

October 2005

One Sunday morning

Tearing myself away from the PC I decided that the time was finally right to take that walk. The one I have been promising myself for five months, since the start of the season.

And so here I am in the shade of a Mediterranean Holly Oak, sitting on the wall of the courtyard of Ag. Paraskevi – the small church on the lower path from Chorio to the road that leads to Roukoniotis. I am looking down over the valley behind the harbour and Yialos, a long way off to the right; the mountain is behind me.

What's going on up here at this time of day?

The wind is in the trees, a mild breeze with the occasional harder breaths. It cools the sweat on my back. I can hear a sheep, it is somewhere on the opposite hillside, invisible. Ah, there is the clock bell at Ag. Triatha, it is half past ten.

That was a bull frog, I am sure of it! A deep, loud croak from behind me, close by. Even more confusing is the sound of an owl. It makes the same sound as the owl that sits on the telegraph wire at night outside the house. Maybe this one is on its way back home from a very late night at wherever owls go to party on a Saturday night. Unperturbed by the owl, a finch explores the tree above me and far away I can hear the distant sounds of human life – an anchor chain is being dropped into the harbour.

Another sheep bleats. A distant goat bell.

Two ramblers pass, stop for water and a chat then they're off for a swim at Vasilios. As soon as they leave, the bells at Triatha start their slow, two tone (minor third for the musically minded) toll, announcing a funeral. The wind picks up and I realise the date, September 11th. My mind wanders back…

Four years ago:

I was driving home from Hastings when I heard the news on the radio and didn't believe it. It sunk in when I saw the television reports; believing my eyes and not my ears.

Three years ago:

I was looking for a permanent rental property on Symi while staying at Lemonitisa studio. We had only been on the island three days and Neil was already working at the Windmill.

Two years go:

I was working for Takis in the leather shop. Walking from the house near Triatha (top of the village) to the other side of Yialos and back again, every day, seven days a week for over seven months. I was two stone lighter in those days. (Quick calculation: roughly 500 steps from work to house x 231 days = 115,500 steps climbed in one season.)

One year ago:

New house, new website and working in the Rainbow bar in the afternoons – just like the present day.

A cockerel brings me back to the here and now – cockerels don't wear watches around here and go off all day and night. A sparrow in the tree. A motorbike growls up the hill – get those baffles fixed boy! It's baffling why they take them out and want to make their bike sound louder than everyone else's. But you know what they say: the louder the motorbike the smaller the… personality.

The Castro bell has joined Triatha now, news of the funeral is spreading.

I notice some graffiti on the wall: $M + S + A = II$. Is this the formula for turning base metals into gold left by some long ago alchemist or a recipe for a youthful ménage a trios? It is old graffiti, the moss has grown over it in parts.

Some leaves on the nearby trees are turning brown, autumn is coming; to be quickly followed by winter.

"What do you do in the winter?"

"What's it like here in the winter?"

Shall I write the book that answers these more than frequently asked questions? If I do I can refer daily enquirers to the appropriate pay and download page on the website. I think I might.

"What do you do in the winter?"

"I write a book called 'What do you do in the winter' which you can buy for €9.99 – you'll find all the answers you need…"

More bells, goats, sparrows in the breeze-ruffled tree. A motorbike way down in the harbour a mile away.

It is nearing lunch time. The rocky path beckons me down, back through the upper village, through the ruins and bells, new houses and people to home.

I notice that the sea has goose-bumps.

November 2005

I'm honestly thinking of writing that book: "What do you do in the winter?"

I sat down the other day to make a start and something completely different came out. It's kind of based on the idea of describing what everyone here gets up to during the winter months but with a twist. It's also a way of learning some new and unhelpful Greek words. Now don't fret, you don't have to be able to read Greek to understand what's written below as I have very kindly put the Greek words in Latin characters. (You don't need to be able to read Latin either, just the alphabet.)

You might find these abbreviations helpful though:

Abbreviations:

a., adjective

f., feminine

fam., familiar

i., intransitive

lit: literal meaning (as taken from the pocket Oxford Greek dictionary 1995)

pl., plural

s., substantive

vb., verb

So here are a few Greek words, their Village View meaning and their actual meaning. Hopefully you'll get my drift as you read on and hopefully, if you are a fellow ex-pat, you won't take offence.

1 Apithanos

An ex-pat will read this, recognise him/herself and be so happy about what I've written and take so little offence that he/she will buy me dinner.

Apithanos (lit: a. Unlikely.)

2 Taktikos

Boats can be unreliable. Or rather the weather can be which makes the boats subject to changes in timetable and cancellations.

Taktikos (lit: a. Habitual)

3 Ksephouskono

The sound of someone from Symi realising that they are going to be stuck in Rhodes for five days as the ferry has been cancelled and they only came over for a morning's shopping.

Ksephouskono (lit: vb. Deflate)

4 Lipothimo

What that person does at the end of the five unexpected days in Rhodes when they get their hotel bill.

Lipothimo (lit: vb. To pass out)

5 Anakouphisi

The feeling of finally getting onto the ferry after five winter days in Rhodes and heading for home.

Anakouphisi (lit: s. f. Relief)

6 Ektrochiazomai

What you do when the ferry gets within six inches of the quay before pulling out again as the captain decides it's too rough to dock in Symi after all.

Ektrochiazomai (lit: v. i. go off the rails - (go berserk in other words, not leap from the stern rail – although that can be tempting at this time.))

7 Loutsa

The act of being caught in a light rain shower on Symi.

Loutsa (lit: s.f. fam. Get drenched)

8 Avolos

The sound of water in your Wellingtons while walking down to the supermarket.

Avolos (lit: a. Uncomfortable)

9 Enochlitikos

When everyone in the supermarket looks at the water sloshing from the tops of your Wellingtons as you queue to buy bottled water.

Enochlitikos (lit: Embarrassing)

10 Aschimos

The last few tomatoes left in the supermarket when deliveries by sea are held up.

Aschimos (lit: Unsightly)

11 Anagaios

The annual unpleasant custom of getting one's pleasure boat out of the water for the winter.

Anagaios (lit: Necessary. Also colloquial: W.C.)

12 Pliksi

A discussion group for ex-pat small boat owners.

Pliksi (lit: Boredom)

13 Aniaros

The annual unpleasant custom of putting one's pleasure boat *back* in the water after the winter. Usually involves two four-wheel drive vehicles, a borrowed trailer, several gin and tonics and a lot of liaison with the Pliksi.

Aniaros (a. Tedious)

14 Soupa – moupes

A warm greeting at a November cocktail party, as in: 'darling you look soupa!' (soupa = soup and the conversation that follows the greeting is known as soupa-moupes.)

Soupa – moupes (lit: Chatter about this and that. Literally lit: you tell me soup.)

15 Stratefsimos

A newly arrived ex-pat desperately hoping not to fall in with the Gin & Tonic crowd who do little but Soupa-moupes about the Pliksi and Aniaros.

Stratefsimos (lit: a. Liable to conscription)

16 Anapophefktos

An invitation to dinner at the home of someone you wouldn't normally want to spend time with but who is one of the few people left on the island in January who speak the same language as you.

Anapophefktos (lit: a. Unavoidable)

There, that's enough for now. If I ever start and/or finish the book, "What do you do in the winter?" I'll let you know when it goes on sale, it will be an e-book. Oh, I can just see the hoards of eager would be e-book buyers queuing all night outside their computers to get their hands on a first edition electronic copy. Yelios – (*a. Absurd.*)

December 2005

Now then, I'm not too sure what this is about, except that I know it's about what I saw on TV last weekend. Friday night to be exact. To be even more exact it was during a film that was on at about 10.00 pm on Friday and to be even more… you get the picture, it is the adverts that I want to tell you about.

But first:

I was watching a video the other night, something recorded a few years ago in England complete with English adverts. (Very polite, to the point and not too many of them, as if the advertisers don't really want to interrupt your televisual enjoyment of *Murder she wrote* or similar.) But watching old recordings is always a double edged sword. It's fun to see the old ads and the old programmes but a bit frustrating when the announcer announces afterwards that next week they will be showing something you'd love to see - and then you realise that you're about five years too late and you missed it.

But at least in the UK the adverts don't go on for 20 minutes, or start five minutes into the show, or leap back in two minutes before the end of the show. Very often you wait during the 20 minutes advert break just to catch the last line of a film and the credits, and even then the credits get interrupted by the list of programme sponsors so you never know who "what is his name?" or "I recognise her" are, after racking your brains through the entire film trying to remember. At least that's how it happens on Greek TV – the Star channel in particular.

During two – only two – advert breaks in last Friday's film I counted no less than fifty five advertisements. 27 in the first break and 28 in the second. The most I've counted in any one advert break was 35, (including trailers for other films and programmes.) I didn't know there was so much to advertise. Well, there is. Now, bearing in mind this was late-ish on a Friday, so we didn't get the ten minute long Laser Line docu-ads that are like Oliver Stone epics in themselves, here's a breakdown of what we were being sold during a (bad) James Bond film:

8 Cars - various makes and models

7 Shopping malls and electrical shops

7 Phones, mobiles and networks

7 Varieties of food including chocolate

6 Newspapers/magazines

5 Different kinds of alcohol

5 Trailers for other films and theatre shows

3 Varieties of cosmetics

2 Books

2 Banks

1 New house

1 Lottery

1 Condom

    I never got to the credits to find out the name of that very famous actress playing Bond's girlfriend in the swimming pool. Such is the power of advertising that, by the time the film finished, I was already out searching for a new car to drive to the mall where I could have chocolate while reading my Sunday paper sipping a Baileys and deciding what film to go and see after I'd moisturised, read some Dickens and paid for it all on my new credit card which came free with the new house that I bought with the lottery money I'd won!

    I'll leave the condom to your imagination.

2006
A few random jottings

Medical matters

I was going to let you know all the details of Neil's recent hospital operation but... well, SymiDream's not that kind of site! Instead I thought I'd just mention a few things about the medical services around here. A lot of visitors ask about this when I'm taking my village walks and many are surprised at the answers.

As we pass the Old Pharmacy in the village – restored in the 1950's to its original state – and take a look inside I am sure some people expect our island clinic (in Yialos) to look similar. In fact we're quite up to date on medical matters around here and compared to my experiences in the UK, we're better off.

For a start, Neil's operation. (Nothing major, just your usual "getting near to middle aged and spent a lot of time sitting down" problem.) Having visited a private specialist in Rhodes (consultation for as long as necessary, ultrasounds, good English and no waiting – all for around €60 as we have already seen,) he was referred to the award winning hospital in Rhodes for the surgery. At this point something unusual happened. The surgeon (actually chief-surgeon) phoned to apologise for the wait he would have to endure as a new operating theatre was being built and this had caused a backlog. The wait, as it turned out, was for only six weeks.

Not too bad compared to the UK but a lot longer than the wait another friend had to endure for a hernia Op. He saw the island doctor who diagnosed the problem, phoned the hospital there and then and then asked "when would you like to go in? Is next Wednesday o.k.?" – My 85 year old godfather had to wait 18 months with the good old NHS and got an appointment a week after paying out for a private operation as he couldn't wait any longer.

Anyway, the hospital rang on a Friday and invited Neil in on the Sunday, the op was done on the Monday and he was out on the Friday. His only complaint was the food. Noodle soup with lemon and camomile tea for five days. But it's a good way of losing weight. The wards at Rhodes General have a maximum of four beds, so it's fairly private, but the corridor can be a bit noisy especially at night. The nurses are efficient and don't stand for any messing about, the doctors are succinct and to the point and visiting hours seem to be whenever you want and for as long as you want.

Thanks to IKA and TEVE (health insurance schemes for workers and self employed folk,) everything is paid for and the paper work is surprisingly straightforward.

So top marks for the hospital in Rhodes!

Back on the island we have the new clinic down town and the only grumble I've heard about the staff there is that they tell you off for not coming to see a doctor before you realised you were ill. Prevention is a big thing around here and the 'health books' you need each year to work in bars or restaurants – though a bit time consuming to arrange – are actually a part of the prevention ethos, I feel. You need a blood test and chest X-ray annually to update your book. Again free (or you can go private if you want) and an annual way of checking for anything nasty that might be lurking within without you knowing.

One last thing: if you're on Symi and you have a medical emergency there are a few ways of being dealt with:

Dire emergency – you get air-lifted to Rhodes in about 20 minutes, quicker than phoning an ambulance back home?

Not so dire but still an emergency – a ferry or boat will take you over immediately on a special trip

You can wait till later – the boat will take you when it's next going and someone will take you to the hospital at the other end if you can't get there yourself.

You can wait till you get home – the local clinic will treat you for free and then you can see your own doctors when you get home

But remember – if you are visiting you should always have health insurance or an E111 form (or whatever the latest scheme is) – as being airlifted off is probably very expensive!

So, now we are all fit and healthy again and summer is about to start we can give up smoking, stop drinking so much beer, take more exercise and... What a thought! Quick! I need a valium.

January 2006

Neil writes...

A quick rewind to the relentless heat of mid summer when two young journalists appeared on the island:

They stood in awe as the Symi boat glided into Yialos on still blue water. With childlike enthusiasm they spent the next fortnight doing everything and seeing as much as they could. They came into my photo shop, bought a few cards and went on a two and a half hour walk with James where they listened intently to the talk about the history of the jewel of the Dodecanese, Symi.

Fast forward to real time. January 15th:

I got a phone call from Brian informing me that Jen had e-mailed a copy of a write up that had appeared in the Mail on Sunday; a write up about Symi that included mentions of the shop and James' walk.

A week later and I managed to get hold of a copy (the e-mailed version was too small to read clearly). With a proud heart and nervous fingers I flicked through the paper until I found us on a double page spread. My eyes danced over the writing. It was a good write up – even though they had misquoted James slightly, the British/allies 'invaded' the island in order to liberate it from the German forces etc. And it's my photo shop not James' and Jennine is called Jennine not Jenny but hey ho, it was a good promotional piece and a big thank you to the Mail on Sunday.

Roll on April when I have photos appearing in a Swiss 'homes and gardens' magazine.

A trip to town

A few jobs need to be done today involving visits to some of the most complicated facilities in the harbour: The doctor, the pharmacy and the post office. I allow myself two hours, fortify myself with three cups of coffee and set off into a warm-ish but blustery December morning; the penultimate day of the year.

First stop: the dustbins down by Campos supermarket, our nearest rubbish collection point. Put two bags of rubbish in the paladin.

Second: The shop, to collect some "front cover" photos for people who have ordered them from Neil, to be delivered in the harbour. 1st delay of the day; one of the donkey train guys needs his passport photos taking and I hang about just in case there's a translation problem. There isn't but I can't get out until the donkeys move away from the door which they do once they have had a good browse around the shop.

Third: No trouble on the Kali Strata, all clear, no delays. Bump into Gabbie as soon as I land in Yialos and so can hand over the front cover prints – getting ahead of schedule as…

Forth: I find the doctor's waiting room empty! After waiting for ten minutes and no apparent reason I get to explain that I didn't hand in a prescription within five days of it being written and therefore need a new one. That takes all of five seconds to do and I'm off to the post office.

Fifth: Post office and yes there is the long awaited 'you have a parcel' slip waiting for me in the PO box (with a cheque to be paid into the bank yippee!). Only two priests waiting to be served before me and as I wait, Jenine and Sam come in to collect a parcel so I leave the queue and go to the back room to ask Lefteris if my parcel is in there with theirs. No, it's in the store room so I must go back to the front office. The two priests have now been joined by three ladies and a coastguard so I am seventh in the queue. Decide to come back later.

Sixth: Bank to pay in cheque and lo! No queue! But the transaction still takes fifteen minutes as it's not a Euro cheque but at least, once converted, I have an extra 300 in the bank. Go to the cash machine and take out 300 – swings and roundabouts. But I am running out of time – I have a Bulgarian coming for an English lesson at 11.30 so need to get my skates on.

Seventh: Unscheduled stop for a chat with Nikos at the clothes shop. Slow winter for clothes he says. I don't tell him that a new clothes shop opened the other day in Chorio but rush on towards the Pharmacy and…

Eighth: Stop to check the boat schedule for January as I have to get to Rhodes and then Athens and then England by the 12th. But there is a boat of some sort every day so as long as the weather doesn't turn nasty I should be o.k.

Ninth: Pharmacy at last! Jenine toots her horn (of the car) and offers a lift. There is only one person in the pharmacy so I shouldn't be too long... Ha! One of the things I need will be arriving from Rhodes that afternoon and the other two... well I can only have one per prescription as it's on IKA so I will need to get another prescription to cover it and the fact that the three things together costs more than the allowed limit per prescription means I will have to go back to the doctor to get a new prescription for those two and can I go now? No? (Outraged glare from Pharmacist – maybe because six people have now arrived and are trying to push in. Pharmacy suddenly resembles the Stock Exchange trading room floor.) Come back on Monday? O.k. Ten minutes later (and much thanks to an English speaking Greek lady who filed in the gaps for me,) and I come out with 30% of what I went in for. But the good news: The tablets normally costs 40 euros a packet but IKA pay most of that so I only have to pay 5 – the small tube of cream would have been over 80 by the way, so always have health insurance of some sort if you plan to be ill or have a minor middle-aged-man ailment in Greece.

Tenth: Dear Jenine and Sam are still waiting for me in the car so leap in with fifteen minutes to go before English lesson and zip off up the hill... where Sam's daddy is mixing concrete so a quick pit stop to say hello and then on to the village.

Eleventh: Where I have to pop into the (donkey free) shop to give Neil my mobile as he has left his at home and where there is a till roll crisis... running out... five minutes to lesson time... find another one for him in the store room that is apparently administered by Stig of the dump and dash off home...

Stopping (**twelfth**) to admire the new metal work Paul is putting up for Yianni at the Rainbow bar ('coffee?' 'no time!' 'ah – sigar sigar, coffee' 'later!') before dashing off again, waving vague and brief good mornings to various passing acquaintances and finally getting to the house before the Bulgarian arrives for his English lesson.

Just in time to get a message on Neil's phone, from my phone back in the shop, to say that Ivo has got work today so won't be coming. Realise that it's the end of the month tomorrow and that I haven't written a village view so... well, so here I am and here it is!

PS: Oh – as I will not be back from England until around February 4th (weather and Poseidon willing) next month's Symi Dream updates will be late. You'll just have to slip into GMT (Greek Maybe Time) and be patient.

England

An interesting village view this month as I wasn't in the village for most of January. I popped back to England to do some musical work for a theatre company. Actually my brief was to re-orchestrate Mozart's *The Magic Flute* for deaf children under 7, and I'm not making that up.

As usual a trip to England in the winter requires planning. I'm pleased to say that, by booking in advance with both Aegean (Rhodes to Athens) and Easy Jet (Athens to Gatwick) I was able to secure tickets at a reasonable price. Even better is that you book and buy on line so you don't have to wait for tickets to arrive – just print the details and show them at the airport. There was a bit of doubt over which day I would be leaving the island as it all depends on boats and wind, but in the end I only had to spend two nights in Rhodes in advance of my 7 a.m. flight to Athens.

So what do you do in Brighton between bouts of The Queen of the Night and Pa, pa pa, pa pa pa….? Well, firstly you adjust to the bathroom arrangements. Not having to hold the shower or stand in a bucket, being careful not to use the bathroom bin for used toilet paper and being able to shave with running water. And the shopping arrangements: a car, a car park, Sainsbury's and a shopping trolley – what fun. And then, when settled in and once again used to central heating and dry clothes it's time to go out.

A few things I'd not seen in the two years since I last visited England: Snow, you don't get much on Symi. Traffic wardens. Chewing gum trodden into the street, yuk! Most of central Brighton is carpeted by Wrigley's these days. Frost on car windows. Traffic lights. Theatre: Cirque de Solei – spelling? – at the Albert hall, in a box with Champers and everything! An amateur pantomime which reminded me that we should think about starting Symi Amateur Dramatics (SAD for short) but then there's no need as you get real dramatics daily, and finally Jason Donovan playing Sweeny Todd (Sondheim's version) at the Theatre Royal. Least said soonest forgotten.

I'd also not had such fun in front of a television for a long time. Wall to wall docu-soaps and lifestyle shows. Celebrity Big Brother (Celebrity don't bother if you ask me). A place in the sun, my place in the sun, a place in Greece, a place in the sun revisited, Honey I'm killing the kids (show us your lifestyle and we'll scare you into eating carrots), fat club, fit club, Club Reps, buy a house, sell a house, auction family heirlooms for a new plasma TV… the list goes on, on 60 channels, 24 hours a day. Fabulous!

And then coming home again – always the best bit and made easier this time by a taxi. Unable to sleep I spent the night watching the last of the crap TV and eating the last of the English sausages before getting in a cab at 4 a.m. and being driven to the airport (usually get the last train at 11. p.m. and spend the night wandering the terminal like Tom Hanks). Check in immediately. A couple of coffees and onto a punctual plane. A bit of a doze and there's Athens. More coffee and lunch then a short hop down to Rhodes (warmth!) and another taxi to the hotel where the ideal receptionist arranged my ferry schedule for the next day. Before I know it I'm slipping back across the sea with a huge suitcase full of supplies. (Oxo cubes, gravy powder, four original paintings by mother, two pairs of headphones and a piano – I kid you not) and then it's home at last. All as if nothing had ever happened.

And then I find that the Mail on Sunday has written about Symi, our shop and my guided walks – favourably I am pleased to say. The only down side on returning was the computer business. The old one blew up just after I left the island and Neil had spent three weeks trying to get it fixed – but that wasn't possible – so as soon as I walk in the door it's time to put the new one together, scramble about for the programmes and files I luckily back up regularly and start putting the website back together. All done now and it's back to work.

March 2006

It seems so long ago that March started I can't remember everything that's happened! Or is that because I have been enjoying a relaxed month before the season starts and things get busy again... "possible, very possible."

O.k. so here we go...

First of all there was a carnival in Yialos on March 5th. The schools put on a great show, fancy dress with an Oriental theme (among others) and a stage show complete with Chinese dragons. Much free souvlaki and wine, dancing and generally making merry before...

Clean Monday on March 6th. A few of us went for a picnic up at Stavros Tou Polemou - the highest monastery on the island (and one of the settings for **'Jason and the Sargonauts'** - plug). Later we went to the top of the **Vigla** (the highest mountain on the island) to fly some kites, or rather to have some kites fly us.

The next day there was a church service and parade down in Yialos, March 7th. This happens every year on my mother's birthday but that's not the real reason for the celebration.

Since then there has been much activity both in Yialos and Chorio (and probably elsewhere too) as everyone with a business gets ready for the upcoming season. In Chorio, Giorgio's taverna is getting a new outside roof over the avli while the inside is being painted up. George the butcher has been painting his shop and George the souvlaki shop has got new menus. There, that's done the Georges.

Down the road at the Windmill things are starting to take shape too. There is a new owner this year, Rhiannon has taken on the restaurant and has started work on some outside wind-protection (nothing to do with the healthy menu, but more to do with being a windmill) so diners will be able to eat out in all degrees of the Beaufort scale. She will also have a new waiter this summer - me!

Meanwhile householders are starting to prepare their buildings for Easter, painting the walls with Asvesti and painting the paths in bright colours. It's a time for regeneration as the devout prepare for Easter and the really devout take on the 40 day fast.

Down in the harbour I've caught Takis painting his forecourt at the leather shop, Panormitis has a new display for his sponges, the plastic winter shrouds are coming off the cafes as the weather improves and new paths are being laid around parts of the road. It's all looking good down there. Our new boat The

Proteus (bigger than the Symi but slightly shorter than the Rodanthi - for those of you who study these things) is up and running now making the two hour crossing to Rhodes on a reasonably regular basis and being able to carry trucks and cars.

Yesterday we had an eclipse, partial from Symi but apparently full in Kastalorizo, very strange daylight-moonlight effects for half an hour that I couldn't capture on camera, sadly.

It's all starting to happen so if you haven't booked your holiday already - get to it now!

Let's go shopping!

When there's nothing much else to do in the village on a sunny, but cold, winter's day you can always go out shopping for a day. A whole day? Well, in theory yes…

We start at the supermarket nearest to home, still referred to as Fortini's, or 'the American', or Michaelis' or Fortnums – whatever you call it you always get a friendly welcome from George and Petros. Favourite thing to do in there? Search for the free gifts that come with the washing powder and Mayonnaise.

Then we'll head into the 'high street'. After calling in at Zoi's (in the summer) for souvlakies the next retail outlet we come to is… the souvlaki shop and Noufri's supermarket opposite where we stop for a chat and a glass of something far too strong for that time of day. Actually while we're in the neighbourhood we can pop up that alleyway to visit the ladies clothes shop and the 'German' bakery and if we needed to we could go further to the next little supermarket and beyond to the Pandapoleion – nothing to do with bears but another supermarket, 'Lambros'.

O.k., done them now back to the high street and maybe a quick stop at Glaros for a coffee and a toastie before taking our sewing into Katina opposite. A drink at the Jean and Tonic next door while we wait? Or a browse in the new clothes shop opposite for a wedding dress we simply must have or a nick-nack from George's household store next door? No, I think more bread from the wood-oven bakery, something to nibble on while browsing Michaelis' new stationery and DVD rental shop.

And then it's time for shoes and slippers at the cobblers and a quick bite to eat at Syloggos (when open) before crossing over to the kiosk for a packet of cigarettes and a weather update.

Double back across the 'street' – avoiding the 'traffic' to call in on Katarina in the household goods store for some very ornate vase or similar before calling in at Lefteris' Kafenion for another coffee and toastie followed by a beer and peanuts at the Rainbow bar next door where the TV offers football or Animal Planet.

Pick up a joint (of meat) from the butchers, some nails and other useful D.I.Y. bits and pieces from Petros, order flowers from the flower shop, admire the antiques at the architect's office and stop off to say hello to Neil at SymiDream – get passport photos taken and catch up on the latest digital photo news. Then down to the corner, turn right and up to the hardware store for some paint to whitewash the house with. A quick nose around the '100 drachmae shop', pick up some bathroom tiles from the tile shop, call into the next supermarket and get some new clothes and a bicycle from the shop on the corner.

Lunch is tempting at The Windmill but it won't be open until the summer – under new management – so make do with a drink at the Micro café. Again in summer it would be possible to take a room at the Fiona or Village hotels to recover but, as it's winter we'll have to make do with another drink this time at the Sunrise café.

Staggering now – and not just under the weight of the paint, nails, flowers, bread, tiles, clothes, bicycle, antique dresser, limited edition photo, washing powder and so on – we head down the hill to see what the Campos supermarket has on offer and that done, another drink at Ringo's bar. Resist the temptation to head further towards Pedi for a dance at the newly opened Alethani club but instead head back towards the village and pick up more cigarettes and phone cards at the kiosk by the bus stop.

That's taken us almost round in a circle and we have to decide where to go next. We missed the clothes shop opposite the Micro café, so pop back there (via the new flower and garden shop) for something to keep us warm as we head back down the road to 'B&Q' another supermarket on the way to Pedi. Getting hungry again so back up to Georgio's Taverna, eat too much and so nip up to Irenie's clothes shop for something bigger around the waist. Realise that fashionable men's clothes only come in a size 24 waist and am wasting my time.

After lunch we find ourselves with time on our hands so decide to visit the old Pharmacy to check in with the village doctor, the three or four carpenters, the three schools and one technical college, the museum, the two graphic/web designers, the old man who puts your back right for you, the midwife, the private language school and any number of builders, painters, mechanics and plumbers before heading home for a well earned rest.

And if anyone else asks me this summer 'but what do you do in the winter?' I'll refer them to this page!

(I must have forgotten someone so apologies if I have, and not all of these restaurants and hotels etc. are open in the winter.)

April 2006

Neil writes…

It's April and the sun is out, yet it's still not warm enough to be in shorts. The island is the greenest we've ever seen it and full of all kinds of wonderful exotic plants. All around the island, people have woken up from their sleepy slumber of winter and everyone is getting ready for what promises to be a busy summer. You can't walk anywhere without seeing somebody with a tin of paint in one hand and a paint brush in the other.

At the beginning of this month you can hear the occasional bang in the distance and it gets closer and louder with each passing day. Easter is on its way and before you know it the island is rocking with the big drums of dynamite being set alight up in the hills. My Dad and brother are here for a week's holiday and my dad is wary after one loud bang makes our windows and doors shake and the cat goes flying six feet in the air with shock. Impressive fireworks light the night sky to a chorus of 'ooos' and 'ahhhs.'

Handy hints for working legally on Symi

Having now spent four seasons here I'm at last starting to get a vague idea of what you need to do to work legally on Symi. You might still find this interesting even if you don't intend to live and work here - so read on anyway.

Firstly there seems to be great confusion about green cards, (residency permits). I went to the police station last year to get a new one and it was relatively hassle free. The chief of police filled out the forms with me, accepted my four small photos and then sent me away to fill out a barely legible form that had already been photocopied to death and make five copies. Luckily my accountant produced a new version, already filled in and copied five times so that was even easier. Back to the police station for the final checks and to dare to ask the question; "as I am a European citizen with an E.U. passport, do I actually need one of these?"

Answer, "no". You are supposed to register with your local police station within 3 months of arriving in Greece from any other country (if you are staying longer than three months) but if you are an E.U. passport holder that's all you need to do. The chief did mumble something about the IKA department needing the card if and when I claim IKA so I got him to issue me one just in case. Later I found out that other non-Greek folk are happily claiming and receiving IKA without having a green card so I still have no idea why some folk on Symi still say you need one, maybe they are still living in the pre-Europe days, maybe they enjoy unnecessary paperwork or maybe they just like spending time with men in uniforms.

Anyway - this year I am not getting a green card and the accountant has checked with IKA and they say they don't need to see one. If that turns out to be untrue then some European Court will be hearing from me.

Note: early 2006 a law was passed. Lo! European citizens do not need a green card to work in Greece anymore. Official.

IKA, by the way, is health and unemployment insurance for workers, a bit like national insurance in the U.K. Your employer pays your contributions and you are covered for health care after the first three months of paying. After working *two* seasons (or a minimum number of days per year - 125) you are then entitled to unemployment payments in the winter. It's a bit like working a year in hand, except it's not because if you take a break and don't work and pay contributions for a year/season/125 days then you start from scratch again and have to work another two years before receiving unemployment benefit.

This is going to get complicated now so pay attention!

Here are some notes and thoughts about my IKA experience:

Make sure your job comes with IKA contributions. Some employers will say things like, no IKA - in which case you go and work somewhere else.

Some will say you get IKA and then don't pay it for you. Some will say you get IKA and they pay it but you get a crap wage in return. Others, like all the Greek people I have so far worked for on Symi, will pay you a reasonable wage and make your contributions as they should. Some will even get their accountant to do as much of the paperwork as possible on your behalf. (Thanks Nikos and Takis!) It is kind of possible to pay your own IKA contributions but you still need to be on an employers' books.

Make sure your employer is actually paying it - there is a book/paper you sign to show that it is being paid. You will also get an IKA number (mine is a 7 digit number,) this is vital so make sure you are told it and keep a note of it. In fact keep all paperwork in a file and don't lose any of it. Ever.

You must go to the local Tax office and register as a tax payer too - they issue you a tax number, which sounds like 'Afimi' as it's made up of three Greek letters •, •, •, Alpha, Fi and Mi. My A• • number is 9 digits long. (And I'm not just showing off.) We went with an accountant to get ours done and it certainly helps to be able to speak Greek in hell holes like the Rhodes tax office. He got us a form, showed us what to write, where to sign and then stood us in the right queue. Didn't take too long. He also went and sorted our IKA numbers out as the IKA office is also a bit of a nightmare.

Big tip: It's worth paying a good, local accountant to do the dirty work for you, particularly in your first years. Unless you speak Greek more than fluently, like queuing and/or are good at pushing in.

Back to IKA. Keep all IKA 'stamps' (pretty pieces of paper with a hologram stamp on them) that IKA send you towards the end of the season. You need these to claim your benefit later on.

ATOMIKO • IB• IA• IO • • EIA• . What on earth…? Person's Health Book (number 1). After working for a while and having your IKA paid you should receive an IKA 'doctor's book' - this shows that you are covered, the doctors make notes in it and you only pay 25% of the prescription fees. (Medicines are very expensive so this is a vital book if you are planning to be ill.) It also ensures you don't pay for hospital treatment. If you are travelling in Greece as well as working, always take your IKA book with you, or at least your number.

ATOMIKO BIB• IA• IO • • EIAS. Again? Yes, actually I should have told you about this earlier. If you are working in a café, bar, restaurant etc. serving the public with food and drinks then you need a Person's Health Book (number 2). There is still some debate about whether you need this book if you are working in a shop. My microbiologist and accountant say you don't, other people say you do. The book itself isn't a problem, it costs €1.00 from a stationery shop. The problems start when you have to get it signed by the doctor. Here we go:

Procedure one: (Recommended for masochists only) Boat to Rhodes and stay in a hotel over night. Taxi to hospital by 9.00 a.m. (or somehow get to Rhodes that day before 9.00 a.m. - sometimes possible.) Register for your tests. Queue and get a chest X-ray. Queue and get a blood test. Queue and do a poo test if you are working cooking food. Yuk. Rest of the day at leisure in the delightful city of Rhodes. Stay overnight in a hotel. Return to hospital the next day for the results. Queue etc. Get hospital GP to check tests and sign the book or return to Symi with papers and see the local GP.

Costs per person based on a single room with no supplement: Boats approx €26.00, hotel (with Symi folk winter rates and a lot of poverty pleading) €50.00, taxis €16.00, basic meals and entertainment €60.00. Total: €152.00 not including impulse buying at Marks and Spencer. Cost of tests and paperwork: FREE!

Procedure two: (Highly recommended.) Check that the Symi X-ray machine is working and staffed. When next in Rhodes for something else combine your trip with a visit to a private microbiologist, there's a good one opposite the Plaza Hotel. Get a blood test done and either collect the results later, get someone else to pick them up for you next time they are in Rhodes or ask for them to be sent or faxed to you. Take results to the Symi clinic and wave your health book while asking for 'Photograph*ie*s' and pointing at your chest. Go topless in front of the tall doctor and get the x-ray done. See the GP on duty and show him/her your blood test results and tell him/her you just had your x-ray. (Tall doctor pronounces all is well by shouting 'endaxi' (o.k.) down the corridor - saves printing plates or something.) Helpful doctor updates your book and signs and stamps the appropriate pages.

Costs: Microbiologist €40.00, trip to Rhodes - well I was there anyway. X-rays €0.00. Total: €40.00

Procedure three. (Not recommended at all and I didn't write this,) try and bribe a medical official who has the correct stamp and a willingness to be struck off and share a prison cell with you.

So what are the stages of becoming a legal worker? Here's a check list (correct as possible as at April 2006)

1. You have registered at the cop shop within three months of arriving - suggested
2. You have chosen the Green Card option or not - entirely up to you it seems
3. You have your tax number - vital
4. You have you IKA number - vital
5. You have a job or a job offer (I hope, otherwise you've come this far for no reason!)

6. You have checked that your employer is, or will be, paying your IKA and has registered you on their books - vital
7. You have had your medical checks (if needed) and the GP has signed your health book - vital if you want to be legal and avoid fines later when the police come and check
8. Your other health book (landscape, blue with your IKA number, name and location written on the front,) has arrived and has a paper on the inside front page stating the period of your entitlement - one year. - vital if you need medicine or treatment.

Now you are free to work legally in Greece! Oh - one last thing: Stages 5, 6, 7, 8 and 2 (now defunct) are annual events.

Bravo and kali doulia!

May 2006

A quick list of what went on in May:

Koukoumas happened up at St. Thanasis church in the village – (the unmarried girls of the village traditionally discover their future husbands by way of singing, dancing, silent water, a ring and a dream. It's a long story.)

Neil got the gallery up and running and he's now exhibiting at what I call the "Symi Modern" with three artists currently exhibiting there.

The Windmill restaurant reopened under new management – it's now a mezethes restaurant, serving individual and very tasty dishes. It has been very busy and is a great success, and I know that because I am working there and have lost almost a stone in weight already due to the running around.

The season is up and running and it's work, work, work for all of us! But there is also some social time as old friends return and new friendships are made. I had 11 people on the village walk last Tuesday, braving the unusually hot May weather. (Even the weeds in the garden are struggling.)

We've had live music at Lefteris Kafeneion, the first of the 'posh yachts' in the harbour – a government minister has visited already – the Mayor of Kos has been for a drink at the Rainbow Bar, the birds have had babies and the air is filled with bird song.

The apricots are almost ready, maybe another three weeks, figs are starting to come out on the trees in the ruins, the cats are finding new and various places to doze in the shade.

We've had lunch at Taverna Zoi, live bands at the new Aletheni club, real SAGA-nauts at the Pedi Beach hotel and artists painting on the steps outside the shop. Basically everything is back into summer mode and winter seems like a distant memory already.

I have no idea what to write about this month so it's going to be random thought time - whatever comes out comes out.

It's been a month of sleepless nights. Due mainly to the rise in temperature and having to adjust to the sound of the fan going all night - no air conditioning here. It's also that time of year when the cold water comes out hot from the tap – the cold water pipes go across the flat roof so they heat up pretty quickly. At least I don't have to use the hot water so much. You take a shower and by the time you're dry again you're wet again from sweating. Lovely. The temperature has been in the high 30's I'd say. (Late June – early July)

Why do the cockerels on Symi crow constantly? And why does Lefteris from Syllogos make the same noise when people are trying to eat?

Football fever grips the village with Rainbow acting as the Stand or the Terraces or whatever it's called.

We had a friend visiting in June and so I took a proper day off complete with Laskarina day out. A visit to Stavros tou Polemou (the cross of the war) church up the mountain (read Jason and the Sargonauts), then some time at Panormitis and the boat back. Lots of lazing in the sun drinking too much Retsina, I was in danger of becoming amusing. A day off really takes it out of you - I was knackered the next day.

Which was when our neighbour opposite started revamping part of his house. We now have a small building site on the wasteland in front of our place and dust flying about when the wind blows. The pneumatic drill starts dead on eight every morning followed by sledge-hammering sound effects that last all day. So could be a few sleepless siesta hours as well as nights for a couple of weeks.

Election time is looming and the Mayor has asked for ideas from the non-Greeks as to what a new administration (or the existing one) can do for us. I am going to suggest a few things like: instructions in English as to how to get IKA and tax requirements sorted out; can the town hall put pressure on the ministry of culture to open the Sala (the restored mansion house at the museum); and a few other things I've not thought of yet.

That's enough randomness for one day. I'll try and think of something more interesting for next month, honest.

June 2006

Neil writes…

It's the 4th of June. I had been asked to do some photography on St Nikolas beach by the owner. It was a beautiful Sunday morning so I didn't mind having to close my shop for a couple of hours. He was paying me for my time anyway. I started off slowly, meandering down to Pedi where George, the waiter from Georgeo's, took me on his taxi boat to St Niks. I realise how lucky I am doing the work I do as we sail over the warm blue sea. Once I get to my destination I realise he needs people in the photos and so far there is only me and a couple of others on the beach. I shrug my shoulders and decide to take the whole morning off from the shop and get in a bit of sunbathing whilst I wait for the hoards of people to arrive. A lazy click of my camera here and there for a while, a spot of sunbathing, a coffee and one beer later, more and more people began to descend on the beach. Another few clicks. Lunch with a few friends, another beer, to help my lunch go down, of course, and before I know it, I'm tanned, full up, a bit merry and I'm back on the boat heading towards Pedi again, and it's only two o'clock in the afternoon.

The sun was beating down and the bus had broken down so I walked slowly up the hill. As soon as I was back in Chorio I went to the Rainbow bar knowing James would be working there.

'You look knackered,' he said as he watched the sweat pouring off my face. 'Sit down and I'll get you a drink.'

Feeling relieved, I sat down. The time was now three fifteen.
'Yianni should be back at four o'clock today as he left early, so you may as well wait for me to finish and we'll leave together,' he suggested as I took a refreshing drink of my third beer.

By 4.30 there was still no sign of Yianni so we decided to stay until 6 o'clock when I would go straight to my shop and James to the Windmill. Drink number four turned up and I was definitely feeling the effects of the alcohol and the hot sun by now.

'Yashou Yianni.' I slightly slurred as Yianni turned up just before five.
'We've still got another hour before work,' James says with a grin, 'Time for one more.'

Other people, and friends had arrived for a drink by now and we we're having a really good time. In the midst of laughing I heard a young voice in Greek ask where the photographer was.

'I'm here,' I said as I turned round to see who it was. 'You have to come to my house,' the ten year old boy said, 'my mum's getting married.'

'Okay, when is she getting married?' I asked.

It was, by then, 5.30.

'6 o'clock,' he said looking at me as if I was a fool not to know. 'What, Now…Today!?' I said feeling the panic begin to rise. 'Yes, we have to hurry.'

You have to take note here; nobody had ever mentioned a wedding to me before. It had not been booked and if I hadn't been sitting there, (and had gone home like I really should have,) they would have had no photographer.

I ran down to my shop in a fluster, quickly downloaded the photographs I had taken earlier, grabbed spare batteries, and swapped shirts with James as he was wearing a clean white one.

An hour later, after photographing the bride in her house, I was far up in the mountains, inside a tiny church called Agios Dimitris, clicking away and feeling totally sober and very bewildered about the whole thing. Another hour later it was all finished and I was in the Windmill having a carafe of white wine and about 100 cigarettes and not believing the day I had just had. I still managed to put in an hour of washing dishes at the Windmill though.

Two days later the new bride had her photographs presented in a lovely wedding album. All her family and friends, including herself are raving about the pictures I took and keep coming in telling me how beautiful they are. Extra prints have already been ordered.

Earworms and Wags

Earworms: it's now officially in the dictionary, so I hear. Earworms are those annoying snippets of tune you get stuck in your head and can't get out. I wake up most mornings with an earworm delving about inside the void. In one week alone I've woken up with:

"Black boys are delicious," from Hair; "You'll never walk alone", Carousel; "London Pride," Noel Coward; "Another ditch in the road," Savage Garden; Shostakovich Symphony No. 5, 1st movement, (all of it) "The wheels on the bus go round and round," and something quite unprintable from Jerry Springer The Opera.

My subconscious taste is clearly eclectic. I find the only way to exorcise the earworms is to sing the burrowing annoyance out loud, which isn't a problem with "The wheels on the bus" but was hard going with the Shostakovich. And I don't think the neighbours appreciated the Jerry Springer: "Put your ******* clothes on, you stupid ****."

And talking of stupid ****s: now for the **Wags.**

Apparently WAGS are much in the English 'newspapers' these days. A revue company in England has commissioned me to write a short sketch, including two songs, about WAGS. They had to explain to me what a WAG is, apparently it's a top football player's wife/girlfriend/latest female hanger-on. I had to research on-line as I've not seen a copy of the Sun for... oh, days. (Neil gets one when he goes to Rhodes, brings it back lovingly and I put it in the laundry basket until it turns yellow. The laundry basket is in the bathroom so the 'newspaper' is always on standby in case we run out of...) So I was looking for suitable songs to rewrite lyrics for, hence the My Fair Lady research instead of watching the cup final. (See July's update.)

I've had some preliminary ideas for changed lyrics. Sing along, make up the rest and pray you don't fall prey to an earworm:

"In Hertford, Hereford and Hampshire, *Hintelligence* hardly ever happens." (Apparently Beckingham Palace is in one of those counties)

"All I want is a football jock,

Some young chip off of some old block.

With one enormous...chair."

"When Wayne's in Spain the team goes down the drain," - not sure if that's going to be crude enough, or is even relevant.

I am also trying to track down the Mary Poppins soundtrack:

"Super scally Wags in lipstick let's be all ferocious

Wearing skin tight leather jeans and acting all precocious,

Flash your b**bs occasionally, you'll never go unnoticed

Super scally Wags in lipstick - something quite atrocious!"

Sadly I still don't know enough about footballers' wives, WAGS and the footballers themselves so I need to do more research. But it's a start.

Oh hell! I've now got Dick Van Dyke in my ear: "Gawd blimey Maary Poppins. Chim chiminey, chim chiminey, chim chim chi Rooney!"

July 2006

So what's new and what went on in July?

Well, big news in the village square: the Rainbow Bar now has three fans! Not the scarf waving, anthem chanting variety - I'm sure all the bars up here have those kinds of fans, but I mean the electric variety. Yianni has also put up some bamboo screens to shield punters from the late afternoon sun. All in all, the place is much more comfortable and you now wonder how you ever survived without these latest mod-cons.

In the gallery we have new exhibiting artists, local folk of course, Greek and non-Greek, which is great. We are still working on the hangings - of the paintings I mean - and have received advice and picture hooks from mother in Penzance who knows about these things. We'll get around to it some day but meanwhile you can still view the artwork for free and even buy some original work if you wish.

The World Cup did not go unnoticed of course and we've had regular football nights not only at Jean's but at the Rainbow and Lefteris' kafeneion too. The final was particularly busy apparently, (I was at home watching My Fair Lady as I have to write a comedy sketch about footballers' wives - see July's Village View.) So great times have been had by all... football fans at least.

Oh! More exciting news in the village: the new stationers shop now sells foreign language newspapers. I don't mean the Sun and Sunday Sport, though they do seem to be written in a completely alien language these days, (what are Wags, Chavs etc.?) but quality papers. I spotted a Times and several other sensible looking, non-English publications. The new shop is just up the lane from the square heading towards Zoi's Taverna. The building has been brilliantly restored with some of the finest wood carving we've seen on the island.

As if electric fans and foreign newspapers weren't enough advancement for the village/island, get this: we've now got ADSL internet connection. Before we were stumbling along on ISDN at a whopping 64 kbs a second + dial up fees. Now we're on the basic ADSL package at around 400 kbs at a set fee each month. No need to worry about what time of day you check your emails or upload your website now, you can stay glued to your browser all day if you want.

But why would you when you have the whole island, the social life, the characters and the sea at your disposal?

The festival has started with a gala performance (see Symi Visitor for the news factor) and a fabulous firework display - don't you just love election year, no expense spared. Neil's children visited for a two week break and charmed everyone, so I was busy in the shop while they holidayed on boats and beaches.

Although July is traditionally a 'quiet month' the day boats have arrived with regularity bringing people over from Rhodes and there are enough visitors staying in the village to keep everywhere more or less busy enough. Things tick over as the temperature stays relentlessly high and 'zesti pali' becomes a daily exchange. (Hot again.) We look forward to August…

Panagiri in the mountains

I meet Aruni at the Village Hotel at 8.50 and we're straight into a taxi and soon heading up and out of the village towards Xisos. Turning onto the rough, concrete and rubble road we arrive at 'The church of the Panagia of the Myrtles' a few minutes later. There are already many people sitting outside near the door of the small chapel and a few inside as we quietly enter, light candles and leave while the priest and his helpers continue around us.

We take up seats a little way off, under a Symi oak tree. Friends greet us, I am introduced to strangers as a photographer and computer teacher and I sit drinking ever warming water as Aruni goes to chat with people and later take communion. I can see down into the valley to the west onto the monastery of Michaelis Roukoniotis and over the sea to Datca on the Turkish coast. A breeze is blowing up, welcome on such a hot day. It is August 15th. The sea is calm and the hills around me are dotted with farms and trees, but horribly severed by a new road leading to Toli.

Aruni returns and tells me of Panagias gone by when the whole family would be up here for days before the day of Assumption. She remembers being here as a child when everyone slept at the small house outside of which the cars now park. In those days the boys would sleep the nights outside and the girls would be locked inside the house for the night. Locked, mind you. The next day the service would be held - as it is going on now - in the morning, later they would sleep under the Symi oak tree at lunchtime with the smell of coffee wafting down from the house and in the evening there would be dancing, feasting and music. But not this year; someone has put a stop to it (though I was here two years ago for the evening festivities) and no one is sure who has ordered this, so best not dwell on it.

The priest comes out to bless the congregation, myself included even though I am the only non-Greek person here. Here's a tip, if you are attending a church event in Greece then bring spare change; it's customary to put in a little for a candle and as the collection plate is now brought around, for the collection and blessing. It all goes to help maintain the church and pay for the goodies we will be having after the service.

Now there is only the sound of the liturgy being sung inside and the wind and cicadas in the trees outside, the congregation stand silently for a while and then sit and continue their disparate conversations. I admire the array of pennants and flags and try and translate some of them; they are red, green, yellow blue or white with dark writing. 'Love each other,' 'The monastery of the Panagiri of the Myrtles,' 'Christ son of God,' the Byzantine flag of the double headed eagle, the Greek flag…

I am distracted in my translations as the Icons are now being paraded. The procession stops at the top of the grounds, in front of the house where the girls were once locked in and a prayer is said, presumably not just for them. Then it moves back down to complete its circumnavigation of the church. Boys and men carry the flags and Icons, displaying them all to the faithful congregation before taking them back inside where the service is completed.

And now it's time to eat and socialise. There is much 'ka tou kronou' being said, (doesn't really translate but it's a wish for good years and many of them) 'Xronia Polla' - many years to you - and much cheek kissing and chatting. I see the Artos - the big round brown loaves being taken into the refectory to be cut into Antithoro (in the singular), the small wedge shaped pieces that are blessed in the 'holy of holies', behind the screen in the chapel. We are offered Boutireva, the round, hard bread rings made with butter in them, milky, sweet coffee in china cups and Akoumia, sticky, sweet and delicious donuts. Everything is offered from baskets and later napkins and small bags are offered out for round two so that you can take away some of these sweets for people who can't be here.

As the morning slowly passes (it is now 11.00) I look back out to sea. I count twenty two boats now in the channel between us and Asia Minor and suddenly a weight is lifted from my shoulders, from my head… the cicadas have suddenly stopped singing and I realise how much noise they make. I actually feel myself relax slightly now that they are quiet; a strange thing to notice but my head actually feels lighter. I can hear children playing on the other side of the church, coffee cups chinking in the refectory, much chatter, a calmer wind, laugher from the other courtyard. As I am offered a small, cream filled cake people start to leave and the cicadas start up again.

I meet up with Aruni (now changed into suitable hiking clothes) and we set off back to the village on foot. Crossing the main road a Xisos we take the old donkey path that will bring us into the top of the village. We stop at the small chapel of Paraskevi, the patron Saint of eyes, for a short prayer before continuing on the path. We can see Yialos way below us as Aruni tells me of panagiries of her past. Getting up at two in the morning for the long walk up to Stavros Tou Polemou when her father had ordered mules for her and her sister; but the mules always walked too close to the sheer cliff edges (there was no road then) and so the children preferred to walk. It all sounds so long ago and so distant that I imagine it all in black and white when in fact it was only forty years ago. But it is like the rest of this morning, apart from the taxi maybe; nothing has changed at the Panagiri for hundreds of years.

August 2006
Neil writes…

Blimey it aint half hot mum. In the four years of living here we have never known it to be so hot. There is no air at all and the garden has turned into a desert. I am writing this on the 28th August, our anniversary of leaving Britain. On reflection it's the best move we've ever made. When we left we didn't have a clue what to expect. Now, four years on I have my own shop and a gallery. I have had my photos in various newspapers/magazines around the world and had my shop filmed it will be shown in a Greek soap opera. Also this month James has had two of his books published at last so we're riding high on a wave at the moment. Thank you to everybody who has supported us since living here.

Also this month has seen a new group of artists get together. It is growing in numbers by the day and so far I think we have about 25 people of all different nationalities join together. The aim of the group is to show our various skills off in various exhibition spaces and to have workshops to allow us to teach other people, especially the children of Symi. The director of the group is a Greek lady called Aruni who is an excellent painter and has sold her paintings in various places around the world and has also taught people before. She has a lot of drive and enthusiasm and has already raised money by selling raffle tickets. The prize is one of her own paintings. The first exhibition is going to be held in my gallery on the 24th September just before the local council elections. The mayor will be here and his opposition as will various dignitaries of Symi. It will start off with a priest coming in and blessing not only my shop but the art project and we are all hoping it will be a huge success. We are also hoping to have live music but that hasn't been finalised as yet. Anything and everything will be on view to the public so if you are here at the time please feel free to pop in and view what the local artists of Symi can produce, I'm sure you won't be disappointed.

Earlier this month James went up the mountain with Aruni to join in the church service to celebrate the Assumption of the Virgin Mary and later that same day I went to the celebrations being held at the Alithini chapel. There was food, drink and lots of dancing which carried on to the early morning hours. I was the only non Greek to get up and dance. It was a very good night had by all and I didn't break my leg this time as I did last year on the way home. I was very pleased with myself.

Reigning cats and dogs

The Laskarina sponsored, Symi Animal Welfare vet arrived last night for his annual week long surgery. The aim is to neuter and check up on as many stray cats and dogs (and tamed ones) as possible in order to keep down the islands' stray cat population. Over population simply leads to more malnutrition, disease and suffering of the animals, particularly the kittens and so the visit is well supported by locals - both Greek and non-Greek.

Volunteers will be doing a variety of things during this week. Some will be scouting around the harbour, boat-yard, Pedi and the village with cat boxes and sardines calling for the strays and tempting them into the boxes like the Child-catcher in Chitty-Chitty-Bang-Bang. Another will then drive the boxes to the surgery where Martin, aided by two or three more volunteers, will check, neuter, treat and otherwise examine each animal in turn. The anaesthetic he gives them also contains a... something which gives them partial amnesia - so he tells me - so when the cat wakes up it can't even remember being caught; this helps to lessen any trauma. (We could all do with some of that from time to time.)

There seem to have been a lot of puppies born this year. One bitch had nine in a ruin near us a few months ago. (I refer to the animal not the owner.) We attended a party the other weekend which we assumed would be a BPAB party (please bring a bottle). Turned out to be a PBAD party (Please bring a dog.) There was a ratio at one point of one dog for every two human guests; many were puppies from the sudden influx but the 'stray' mother of some of them also attended - well, gate-crashed. Our host's farewell of 'you wouldn't like to take a dog with you would...' was met with a 'certainly not!' Remember: a puppy is not just for Christmas. If you are careful there should be enough left over for Boxing day.

Sorry - not much of a dog lover me and I don't subscribe to the argument that just because they are cute when young means you should commit yourself for life. (With the exception of Neil of course. Had to say that.)

But with cats it's a different story. Cats commit to you if they feel like it and one of ours, Pipe, who we'd had since a kitten, has now left home. Or died. Not sure which. In the weeks leading up to her disappearance she'd started to get very grumpy about the food we were giving her. The supermarket had changed its brand to 'Fleshy' (yuk name methinks) and Pipe was not happy at all. She hardly ever ate but remained well fed; leading us to suspect that she'd found someone who was prepared to feed her what she liked - which was tins of Tuna, cheese, peas (?!) and smoked mackerel fillets. And of course, any left over cooked meat as long as there was gravy. In the last few days that we saw her she, uncharacteristically, became very friendly and cuddly and paid us lots of attention - like she was saying thank you and goodbye. And then the last I saw of her she was heading off through the garden just like any other day. Wherever she is I'm sure she's getting better food than 'Fleshy'.

Which leaves us with the feline alarm clock, 'Jack'. Six thirty every morning, if I am not up, then he's at the door shouting 'mama!' I kid you not. It does sound like 'mama', I must teach him 'dada' as I'd prefer that. Jack is deaf, noisy, white and moults a lot which is a pain when you have a dark grey carpet. Oh - and I once got woken up at five in the morning because the television was on. I went into the front room to find him sat on the sofa with the remote control in his paw, the TV blaring and the phone off the hook. (No, honestly!) Not only that but there were two cats with him, one licking his... never mind... and staring at me as if to say 'what's it to you, buster?'

Jack the party animal eh? Takes after his dad.

I'm off now, I have duties to attend to. The master of the house will be wanting his bowl of 'Fleshy' - he's not as fussy as Pipe was.

September 2006

The summer seems to have flown by - as it always does when you get near the end of it. I'm writing this on September 28th and there are clouds that threaten rain and a bit of a strong wind. But this will no doubt be temporary and when the sun breaks through, it is still hot enough.

But what's happened in September that I can remember? Hmm...

Well, the first strong winds came on the 1st of the month, helping to bring down the unusual heat that affected most of August and temperatures returned to normal - at the beginning of the month. Neil's mother left after her two weeks' visit and Yiannis from Lefteris Kafeneion caught a whopping great fish which was the excitement of the village square for a whole afternoon and evening. Unfortunately I didn't have a camera on me but it was almost the size of his youngest son who was holding it up proudly as he showed it off to everyone.

The temperature rose again during the month and when we attended a baptism, to photograph and video it for the parents, the ceremony was held outside in the courtyard of Haritomeni church, in the village. Another celebration occurred - Neil's birthday - and we marked the occasion by working from 9 a.m. through until midnight as usual.

The Taverna previously known as To Klima re-opened, or just opened as it is now called Filos (friend). It is serving mezethes (small, individual plates) as well as some pasta and meat dishes. It's also open at lunch time which is great. We've already been several times, giving ourselves an hour off between 1 and 2 - particularly on Tuesdays when I take the guided walk. The walks, by the way, have been going very well and everyone seems to have enjoyed the mornings. I certainly have.

As you'll see from the galleries ODAS (the Association of Creative People of Symi - the acronym comes from the Greek translation) held its first exhibition on 24th. The event and the group were blessed by two priests and over 100 people attended the event. The exhibition will run until the end of the season.

And finally: it's run up to election time. Jean, Lemonia and I have produced a 'how to vote on Symi' hand-out for anyone living on the island who has not voted before - it's available at the shop or at Jean's bar. The election will be October 15th so more about that next month no doubt. Martin arrived last night - the Laskarina, Symi Animal Welfare vet - and the surgery opens tomorrow. I'm doing vasectomies and the like on Monday morning, can't wait. Again, more in the SAW update next month I expect.

And finally finally - Jason and the Sargonauts is now available in Hardback (see our books department) and the paperback will be out as soon as Gill has designed the cover for me. I hope to have some copies available in the shop next year along with other writings about Symi. Watch this space.

Am off to buy paint for the flat roof - have to re-paint it each year or else the rain comes in and floods the house. Here comes winter...

October 2006

Neil writes…

These are just a few days in October:

I was getting desperate for stock, paper, ink etc. and so, as I'd heard from the supplier in Rhodes that my stock order had arrived, I went over. No stock. Twice this had happened within a week and I was getting really desperate as I had 'the wedding of the year' to photograph on the 8th of October. I got another phone call on the 5th telling me my stock had mysteriously arrived for the third time in a week, so on the morning of the 6th I dubiously set off on the Dodecanese Pride. I had a strange feeling something was going to happen that day but didn't know what. I shook the cobwebs from my head and wiped the sleep from my eyes as we arrived in Rhodes harbour.

As everybody walked off the boat I started to text James and not really noticing anybody, I disembarked. I heard somebody in Greek asking people if they needed a room for the night but I didn't really listen properly. I heard another voice beside me and assumed it was somebody asking me if I needed a room. I mumbled a quick 'no' as I was still trying to text James. The next minute the man had pulled me back forcibly by grabbing my rucksack and waving an identity card in my face.

'I am the police,' he said.

He was in everyday wear. He asked for my passport and went through my bags with me watching. He even asked to look in my cigarette packet. I was polite to him the whole time; well you would be wouldn't you? After a while he let me go and I carried on my way as I was in a hurry. After I had actually *got* my stock (told you something strange was going to happen). I texted James and told him what had happened and that I felt as if I was being followed. I've never felt like that before and it made me feel strange even though I knew I hadn't done anything wrong. I tried to put the feeling out of my head but it just kept nagging away.

After a couple of hours I needed the toilet so I rushed off to the old market place. As soon as I came out of the public toilets I saw the policeman who had searched me earlier speaking on the phone, he looked away quickly. I had done all my shopping by now so I went to a bar and sat outside in the open. I didn't see the policeman again but it had left me feeling I had done something wrong, even though I knew I hadn't. I got home later that day and had just enough time for a shower and a quick bite to eat before James and I went to a meeting of ODAS, the creative people of Symi. I took the minutes of the meeting but we had to cut the meeting short as it was Ian's stag night that night and there was no way we were going to miss it.

The stag night was hilarious as the other men made Ian go round in a white, revealing dress all night. James was sensible and went home about midnight. At 8 o'clock in the morning Ian, his best man and I got home. What a night.

The Wedding day, 8th October

I arrived, (after spending the previous day in bed with major hang over,) at Jenine the bride's house at 9 o'clock in the morning. She was a picture. Curlers in her hair and a nightie on. I could see why Ian was marrying her. The morning continued as people kept coming and going and making sure that nothing went wrong for Jenine. At 12.30 I rushed with James to the house Ian had been staying in and took even more photos, then a quick rush back to Jenine's to take photos of her now fully dressed and looking spectacular in her wedding dress.

The wedding party walked down the Kali Strata with two musicians leading the way. When Jenine and Ian met on the bridge down in the harbour I found it hard to keep my camera still as tears were threatening to overspill. It was a lovely, though quick, registry do and afterwards the 110 or so guests boarded a couple of taxi boats and went to St. Nikloas beach. There Ian and Jenine were 'blessed' by James in a humanist ceremony (he had got himself ordained especially for the occasion). The whole day was perfect and we all ended up in Blooms night club and danced the night away. We wish them our deepest, heartfelt congratulations. They are a fantastic couple.

There I said it. Jenine now owes me 20 euros.

Monday 9th

After telling everybody that they could come and see the photos from the wedding on Monday evening, I went to work early and worked on them all day and only stopped for one hour's break for something to eat. James had to take over for a couple of hours as it was election week and as I was the photographer for the party opposing the mayor, I had to go to every meeting and photograph it all. Got back to my shop with a pile of orders which had to be ready by Tuesday night as a lot of the wedding party were leaving on Wednesday. Closed the shop at 9.00 pm and went straight to the Rainbow bar and started work straight away as it was heaving with wedding guests. 'Phew!'

Tuesday 10th

Another day of non-stop work trying to get everybody's orders ready as well as the photos from the meeting the night before. Worked at rainbow bar again but not quite so busy.

Wed 11th

More orders from the remaining guests left on the island and another meeting in the evening. This time it was down in Yialos and it really was something that wouldn't be out of place in the west end of London. It was a great show.

Thursday and Friday:

More orders and the atmosphere on the island is becoming electric with election fever. Also found out today that there had been a photograph of me in a big national Greek newspaper. It's been a good week.

Sunday 15th – election day

I had the morning off work and James went to the shop instead, but I still got out of bed at 6.30 in the morning. I pottered round the house and at 11.30 thought I would make something good for dinner. We had been so busy we'd completely forgotten to go shopping. There was no food in the house at all. I made a quick phone call to James and half an hour later the shop was closed and we were at Filos restaurant. We noticed the Rainbow bar was closed so we knew straight away we wouldn't have to work there that day. A lot of our friends were drinking outside Bullmas so we decided to join them as the weather was lovely. Two drinks later and James and I, accompanied by Terri went to the local school to vote. Five minutes later and we were back at Bullmas: They had run out of envelopes at the polling station. Half an hour later we went back and put our votes in. We felt really pleased with ourselves for doing our duty and guess where we went afterwards? Back to Bullmas.

Later we went to Terri's house for an ouzo and a game of Trivial Pursuit, (no S). We were really having fun when we noticed the time. I had already planned keeping the shop closed that night but we were late for a party and they were holding off the champagne and caviar until we got there. Later that night, on the way home, dynamite rocked the island and fireworks filled the sky. The elections were over and Lefteris, the mayor, had got in again for another four years.

November 2006

What to do on Symi in November? Well, let's see now...

You can sit out in the sun and catch some rays and generally wonder about the weather. It's been quite mild, after the storms in October and a short cold snap. Most days were warm and there was plenty of sitting outside at home and in the village square to be had. Around the 20th things started to get cloudier with a mist that shrouded the coast of Turkey and even crept as far up as the Pedi valley and the Vigla.

You can work. I finished my seven days a week afternoon shifts at the Rainbow bar on 7th November. Since then I've been hammering the keyboard doing my usual work and publishing the odd book here and there. Neil's been opening the shop, taking photos of houses and people and has taken on a freelance Photoshop job, so we've been busy.

You can eat. Boy can you eat! We've been treated to three roast dinners and cooked one ourselves; we've had a curry and trivial pursuit night; we've even had a Thai curry (thanks Jenine); we've been through just about every kind of foodstuff available in the village and put on about half a stone already. But you need to do that for the cold nights.

Apart from an afternoon G&T at Lefteris Kafeneion we've also popped into the Glaros bar to see how it looks now that Pan has given it a face lift. It's much warmer and more homely in there now.

We've been to the harbour (twice!) to collect mail and pay bills. It's all very quiet down there now with a few tavernas open plus the usual collection of bars and cafes. There's been some talk of boats and what will and will not be running during the winter but it seems that the Proteus is going back and forth most days.

You can plan a holiday and I don't just mean a day in Rhodes, though we need to do that before Christmas. We're looking at somewhere off the coast of Ecuador. We haven't had a holiday for seven years so have started saving like mad.

You can sign on. Yes, for the first time in twenty years I'm officially unemployed. I wasn't looking forward to this minefield of administration and red tape but it all went without a hitch. Stelios the accountant gave me a bundle of papers, I took them to the town hall, Irini went through them, (I think it helped that I could fill most of the three forms out in Greek) she rang Stelios, found the important piece of paper at the bottom of the pile and told me she would ring me when my giro was in. None of this take a ticket and queue up for four hours stuff like the last time I did it in Clapham all those years ago. It was more like going for a chat and took about ten minutes.

You can watch every single DVD that Michaelis has in his shop and then start borrowing and sharing others with your friends.

You can read, write, play the piano (if you have one), enjoy the delights of ADSL broadband internet for as long as you can stare at a screen, you can help people set up their ADSL internet connection, pick oranges, cut back the overgrown rosemary bush, search for firewood, walk in the village, walk in the mountains, have Greek lessons, feed cats, rearrange the living room furniture (still not enough space), clean the house and paint the roof so it doesn't leak as much. Oh – and plan Christmas day; can't wait.

And then, if you still have time left, you can write trivia like this for our website.

And Finally December 2006
A tour around the grounds

Now then, as you have been so loyal in reading my updates and Village Views I thought it high time that I invited you in for a tour of the house and grounds. Grounds may be a slightly overenthusiastic word to use but there you go. Just so you can get the setting it's November 28th, the sun is shining though it's a little chilly in the shadows, and there's a thin haze covering the mountain that filters the sun and gives the island a calm and quiet atmosphere.

So here we are at the front gates. I shan't tell you exactly where the house stands as we want to discourage hoards of well wishers and pilgrims from flocking here with a view to 'touching the hem' and 'catching a glimpse' of us in the wild. But it is situated not far from the 'American' supermarket (which is not American) and the 'German' bakery, (which is not German). Let's just say we are in the middle of the village.

Entering the front gates we find ourselves in the downstairs lobby with our landlord's apothiki (that's store room to you) to the left. The downstairs lobby holds mainly technical equipment necessary for life on Symi. The water meter and stop cock, the electricity box and meter and little used gardening paraphernalia. Down here is also a pile of junk that is one day destined for the rubbish tip. It's a kind of death row for broken chairs, cardboard boxes and garden debris and we won't stay here long. It's a sadistic trait of our house that, having climbed the four hundred odd steps from the harbour, one then has another ten, slightly too high, steps to pant up before reaching the level on which the habited part of the house resides. At the top of these we double back to stand on the 'terrace' which is built over the lobby. From here we can admire the view of Turkey, the sea, part of Nimos island, the neighbour's washing line and a cat's cradle of ubiquitous wires that hang from telegraph poles. On the waste ground in front of us we also have an olive tree, a stray cats' playground and from time to time, goats.

Having noted the view we turn and notice that the front door is beside us. The house was, according to Nikos (husband of Taverna Zoi) who was brought up here, a typical Symi house with two rooms up and one and a sterna down. This front door leads into the old salon (drawing room) but we're going to tour the grounds first and enter the house later so we ignore the door for now and head along the side of the house towards the back. Where we reach the front door – this is Symi after all – which is the door we use to come and go through on an everyday basis. But more later. First we'll climb another five steps and enter upon the garden.

Garden is not an over ambitious words to use though the garden is an over ambitious place. Neither of us are gardeners and as we're not allowed to concrete it all over, we've taken to cultivating a luxurious variety of exotic weeds for most of the year. I like to think of the garden as lying fallow like a field in some four crop rotating agricultural system. Having said that there are parts of it where things grow. For example, let me introduce you to the three pepper plants I have raised from seed. They somehow survive their south facing location, raging summer sun and the forgetful gardener who is tight with the watering can and produce pretty white flowers followed by tiny green peppers. Beside them lives the smallest of the three lemon trees, so this area is kind of the nursery school department. But just beyond, in the corner by the compost heap Paul made for us out of a discarded oil drum, we have the two plum trees and the apricot. The plums always grow so high we can only ever reach a few a year but the apricot is the most punctual of fruiters. June 15th is normally the first day that the apricots start to fall and we get involved in a mad scramble to pick them before they hit the ground and commit mass Hari-Kari in a colourful display of splattering that the wasps queue up to pick over. After two weeks of our rescue mission and the tree's attempts at mass crop suicide all the apricots are gone. Either back to Mother Nature, into Marj's home made jam or to the homes of friends and neighbours.

Next to the mentally unstable (but reliable) Apricot tree is the medium sized lemon tree. This one has a habit of only producing one or two lemons a year but as they are the size of hand grenades we'll say no more about it. Next in line stands the orange tree. Or I should say 'squats' the orange tree. It's rather stocky and takes all year to produce oranges that are only edible when cooked or pulped into marmalade. It redeems itself by producing nice smelling flowers in celebration of my birthday each year though so we shouldn't be too hard on it. Finally, at the end of the line, is the big lemon tree. This one produces loads of lemons ranging in size from ping-pong ball to tennis ball depending on how much water we lavish on it in the summer. Behind all these arboreal misfits are two wayward vines that dedicate their lives to creeping around at the back wall and strangling the trees when they think no one is looking. We generally do something about them when they start encroaching on the washing line and we know when it's time to bring the laundry in because there are leaves growing out of it.

Following the path (now painted grey rather than bare concrete as I had some grey paint and five minutes spare one day) towards the back of the house we pass the bougainvillea that's never quite achieved the status it deserves and remains constantly stunted. Then the rose bush-come-giant redwood tree that constantly flowers, drops leaves and petals and needs culling every couple of months. We have, beside this, a small gathering of mint and a fern that must have come on holiday from some tropical dwelling place and liked it so much it stayed, it's totally out of place. And what's more surprising, is that it lives side by side with the two vines that act as shade over the back/front door below.

Vines always deserve a special mention as they are so useful and yet so complicated. Basically they sprout leaves and sixteen miles of new… well vine I guess, every year and quite frankly they don't care in which direction they develop. The water pump up on the roof was nearly smothered this year and we had to machete our way up the stairs to the garden on many occasions. Every two years they give us grapes, so many grapes that we'd never eat them all. (Don't ask why we don't make wine the answer is simple: it's cheaper, quicker, less complicated and probably better tasting to buy it at €2.00 a litre in the shop.) Besides, most of the grapes grow in places that you can't reach and all kinds of bugs live up there with them. Great green uncoordinated caterpillars that drop off and explode on impact; an alarming diversity of beetle; birds and even cats have been known to make a home up there. And in autumn when the grapes start to go off well, it's a constant rain storm of fruit, pips and other detritus that the hornets chuck out while getting merrily pissed on the fermenting fruit. These hornets live a very debauched life. They fuss around the rotting grapes all day until late afternoon when, completely smashed on the juice, they can't even keep themselves upright let alone airborne. We on the other hand live under constant fear of attack from bleary eyed wasps who can't focus and just blunder about outside the front/back door waiting to be trodden on by someone with bare feet. But all said and done we do get some grapes from the vine before the hornets move in, you can use the leaves for dolmades if you're so inclined, it gives shade in the summer and kindling for the fire in the winter and it helps fill some space on these pages.

Meanwhile back in the garden: just before we reach the steps (we're heading along the side of the house but up a level in the garden here) we have a rosemary bush the size of a small country that blocks out all the light from the window it completely covers. We have an annual hacking down which only strengthens its resolve and it comes back extremely quickly and at twice the size. But it does taste good roasted with potatoes. Once we've reached the steps which lead up to the flat roof and chopped our way through the rosemary on one side and the lemon tree on the other, we mount a few steps and we're on top of the bathroom. There's a wide expanse of flat roof up here with a Heath Robinson kind of pipe work arrangement that meanders around aimlessly until it finds the water pump. These pipes carry water from the sterna to the taps and act as an energy saving alarm clock: You know when summer is coming because the cold water they carry comes out of the pipes hot and we hardly need to use the internal water heater. From the flat roof we get a view of the Vigla, our mountain behind us, the church of Thanasis a little way to the west, then the Castro and over to the East is the Pedi valley and bay.

O.k. We've done the grounds, now how about the house? Back down to the fruit tree department, down again to beneath the vine (now cut back for the winter, ha! That'll teach it) and wait for me here at the back/front door while I just pop in and make sure things are tidy for you.

No they are not but then they never are so come on in and watch where you tread. Now then, the front/back door is actually in the middle of the house so it should really be called the front/back/middle door but let's not go into that. Instead we'll go into the sitting room which used to be the courtyard but is now the main hub of the house. Everything from this room and to the right is an extension, hence the flat roof above, and we'll back track in a moment to the old part of the house to our left.

You will notice, in fact you will not fail to notice, the fireplace over which is painted a mural of a Symi scene. Not by us I hasten to add and I won't name names but it's an original feature that we are not allowed to get rid of. It is so original in fact that the harbour scene it depicts has three galleons sailing in three different directions against and into three different prevailing winds. A small row boat the size of a U-boat is attacking one of these ships and on the shore a giant of a man is doing something extraordinary with a net. The Kali Strata (we assume) runs along the right hand shore towards the police station (which is actually on the opposite shore) under a sky that suggests sunset at noon. Beneath this entertaining piece the island's windmills and the stone circle are depicted in fully working order and vivid colours.

Moving swiftly on you must admire the rosemary bush from the safety of the inside of the property as it taps at the window like something from the Little Shop of Horrors. We take the passage that leads to the very back of the house, passing the bathroom (that used to be the outdoor kitchen) on the right and a display of some of Neil's photographs on the left. The kitchen – to switch the light on click it into the off position – is lit by a skylight that doubles as a shower in wet weather and contains all the mod cons you could ever wish for: the noisiest fridge freezer in Christendom, a cooker (don't use the back left ring or the house an possibly the entire parish will be plunged into darkness), and a pantry that has not been opened since about the time Carter discovered

Tutankhamen's tomb. We daren't open this door for fear that something black and fungal will creep out and engulf the island like the Martian weed in the Word of the Worlds.

So we back track as promised, follow me and keep up at the back there I don't want to lose anyone to the monster in the pantry and take a quick peak in the bathroom. More mod cons in here including a washing machine that works and bath taps that don't. Back through the sitting room that is stocked for the winter months with firewood, games, DVDs, CDs books and washing that won't get dry anywhere else. And now we can enter the old part of he house.

The bedroom is always in a constant state of disarray. In fact it looks more like an explosion in an Oxfam shop than a bedroom. Here we have the mattress, the rest of the bed is upstairs in pieces while we wait for a delivery of new six inch nails to replace the ones that were previously holding it together. We have two wardrobes that appear to have been disembowelled and two chairs and a trunk that strain under the contents that came out of the wardrobes. Ignore that mess and have a quick look up the steep stairs, through the hatch and into the mousandra. It is rumoured that the missing parts of the Dead Sea Scrolls can be found up here just behind the other half of the Rosetta stone and I read once that experts think this is where Agatha Christie spent those missing weeks. If in doubt just ask Lord Lucan who also lives up here quite happily with the passengers and crew of the Marie Celeste.

We have everything in our mousandra that you could ever not want (because I can't throw anything away). Apart from the useless pieces of old bed and hundreds of empty boxes that 'might come in useful one day' we have a collection of 70 musicals, a DVD machine and three heaters that don't work, books never to be read again, clothes we'll never fit into and some very rare species of dust. Obviously tidying the mousandra and throwing things out is one of those projects that we're saving for a very rainy day.

Back down the steps, careful that the hatch doesn't... ouch!... fall on your head, never mind and could you turn the light off? There are two switches, the upstairs light is controlled by the switch that is below the one above it which controls the downstairs light – but at least up is off and down is on even if down is up and up is down. And follow me through a noisy sliding door into the front room. At last! Remember this is the room at the front of the house that has the front door we never use as a front door and was the saloni of the old house.

Beneath a purple chandelier (don't ask, it was here when we moved in) we have a fair sized and airy room that I work in. It's where I am now actually, at my father's old desk hammering away at my forth computer in as many years. We have the piano in here that occasionally gets played and even more occasionally gets dusted, we have my books, an expensive Turkish rug from Iran or somewhere else non-Turkish, a typical Greek uncomfortable sofa that visiting Greek people flock to and enjoy immensely and the dining table for winter use only. At the very front we have the balcony that overlooks the same view as the front terrace but with a little more mountain and Pedi to the right.

And there you have it: A tour of the house and grounds. Now, if you have finished being nosy you can file out through the front/front door (noticing the handy light switches which glow in the dark so that you can find them in a power cut…) and leave as many tips for the guide as you want to while you're leaving. Thanks for coming and have a nice day.

24

24 was started in 2006 and will be, when finished, short notes made during each hour of the day. Notes and observations about what is going on at that particular hour in whatever place I am in at the time, so eventually we will have a whole day in the life of Symi. My style.

3.00 a.m.

Surprisingly lively considering the time - but I did go to bed at 8.30 last night. Brain always works best at this time of day so decide to put it to good use.

Coffee first, but even before that Jack, our deaf, white cat appears from his nightly sleeping spot somewhere in the garden and sleepily asks for food. Coffee on the terrace. Not much to see at this hour: stars, a satellite overhead, a small red dot in the sky - Mars. Streetlights around the village, a lone car heading down the road to the harbour, the outside light under the ever expanding vine. But there is much to hear.

The Sonar Owl - don't know its real name, beeps steadily somewhere in a ruin behind the house. It really does sound like one note of a submarine sonar or other mono-tone electronic gadget. Same pitch, same time gap between pings. A cockerel with no sense of time crows at the blackness. A couple of cats have a scrap around the corner and the slight wind harasses the sleeping olive tree opposite the house.

Occasional breaks in the noise, but the owl keeps beeping. An aeroplane moves mysteriously across the night sky, blinking lights and a far off faint rumble from its engines.

Jack reappears to start his security round. Checks the terrace for spiders and shadows. Finds my shadow on the wall and boxes with it for a while before moving on to check why the front door is open. Nothing untoward going on inside so he takes a nap break on the outside bench, not too far away from me.

Work to be done: inside at the computer, faint hum of electronics and soft clicking of keyboard accompanied by the owl now slightly more distant. Jack appears and sits beneath the desk, always wary of some assassination attempt on the person who feeds him. I suspect he has his own interest at heart.

Website updates completed after a second mug of coffee and a cigarette on the terrace. Still no signs of life other than animals that I can not see. It's too early for bells and the churches are all in darkness, recovering from the recent Easter activity no doubt.

My desk lamp throws shadows across the white tiled floor. Jack is on to it immediately, inspecting under the carpet where he suspects the shadows live.

Outside the streetlamp lights the side of the white building whose porch has not been painted since the last war. Our neighbour's washing blows in the breeze. The owl pings.

Time passes so quickly in large measures, has it really been six months since the last season ended? But time passes so slowly in smaller helpings. Three creeps to four as I contemplate another coffee and Jack decides where to sleep next.

4.00 a.m.

Woken by the sounds of cats fighting outside the house. Try to ignore it. No use. The screams and wails cut through the night at the volume of a fighter jet at take off. I get up and stomp to the terrace, searching in the dark for something to throw. The outside table? Too big. A flower pot? Too breakable… I am just contemplating throwing myself when there is a mad scramble in the bushes and the cats come flying out, one chasing the other. They race off down the lane and silence returns.

But it's too late.

Thirsty and awake now. Return to bed after taking on water, but it's late June and hot. The fan is off, don't want to turn it on in case I wake Neil. Lie there forcing myself to go back to sleep. And then there's that sound we all dread: zzzzzzZZ*Z*ZZzzzzzz – mosquito attack. Wave arms around uselessly cursing the thing. Silence. zzzzzzZZ*Z*ZZzzzzzz – it's back.

'I thought it was funny… he he he he.. malaka.'

Someone is talking in their sleep. Give up on that room and try getting back to sleep on the living room sofa. It's a cooler room. Dozing off when cat jumps merrily on my head. Throw it off. Cat wants feeding, it knows that: *big human moving around at night or early morning = food*. It's wrong this time. Just dozing off when zzzzzzZZ*Z*ZZzzzzzz. Reach for can of environmentally and mosquito unfriendly spray and wave it wildly over my head while holding my breath.

Sweat trickles down my back and a Gilbert and Sullivan song comes to mind: *'When you're lying awake with a dismal headache and repose is tabooed by anxiety…'* The cat tiptoes up onto the back of the sofa to watch over me. Start to doze off. Mind alerts me to the fact that I am falling asleep and I wake up again. Then, before I know it, I am dreaming about cat food.

8.00 a.m.

November 8th and it's Panormitis day. We decide to go to Kokimides. (I hope I've spelt that correctly.) This tiny chapel dates from 1697 and is the second highest monastery on Symi after Stavros Tou Polemou.

We leave the house just after eight in the morning carrying two bottles of water and a camera each. We're wearing jumpers and coats because it's a cool morning even though the sun is out. A few steps up and into Alemena square and we meet Hugo with a small party of walkers. We join forces for the assault on the upper village (because I never can find the top donkey path and Hugo knows where he's going, he could do it blindfolded) and within minutes we are through the ruins and the building sites and I'm closing the bedstead which serves as a gate behind me. The view down to Yialos is particularly outstanding and there are plenty of stops for Neil to take photographs of goats that stand and watch us with an air of polite disinterest.

The top donkey track gives up at about twenty feet beneath the road and there's a scramble involved before we're up on the main highway. Several cars pass us as we stop for water and a cigarette, cars filled with happy pilgrims heading towards various island monasteries named Michael in one form or another. It's Saint Michael's day you see, not just Michaelis Panormitis but also Roukoniotis and Kokimides to name but a few.

We follow the road, Hugo and party are ahead of us now, as it turns and passes Xissos, the small settlement down to our right and then we reach the corner. There's a choice here: we either follow the road and climb up a few hairpin bends or we carry straight on up another ancient path that acts as a short cut and rejoins the road higher up. We take the short cut and catch up with Hugo and co. at the small church of Katerina. Declining an early morning ouzo we press on and before we know it were at the monastery of Constantinos. This is the place where we've enjoyed many a morning drinking coffee and eating prickly pears but today we march on past as the road to Kokimides is now in view. As we reach it Yianni the teacher pulls up in his car and berates us for not phoning him and getting a lift. We explain that we wanted to walk but thank him anyway; perhaps we'll take a lift on the way back.

Regret that decision when we realise how long and uphill this next stretch is but finally we are the bottom of the last part of the walk where the track up to Kokimides leaves the road at the chapel of Saint Barbara – she had something to do with gunpowder, I think she got blown up by her father, I don't remember now. Half way up the track and with the summit in sight Zoi's parents stop their nice and inviting new truck and offer us a lift. We explain that we want to walk up and they look at us as if we're completely deranged but drive on cheerfully. Two minutes later and we meet them getting out of their truck at the top of the road. By this time we're carrying most of our clothing as the sun is hot and we're sweating.

As we sit and recover behind the church we hear the service is on-going. The courtyard is full of people waiting patiently for coffee and festivities and the church is packed with worshipers. We greet and are greeted by people we know and made to feel welcome particularly as the only non-Greek people there.

So there you have it. It is a two hour walk from the village to the second highest monastery on the island. Just thought you should know.

10.00 a.m.

It's 10.30 in the morning and we've walked up to Kokimides monastery for the celebration of the name day of Michaelis Kokimides.

We spend the first hour or so sitting under the tree and smiling and nodding, waving even, to various people we know as the churchyard fills up with families. Children play football behind us, mothers sit and chat while the men are over to the left doing something promising with a barbeque. After the service is finished and we've lit candles and been blessed, we join everyone else in taking sweet coffee and donuts and generally feel good about life. Particularly as the views from up there are wonderful and the sky is clear. It's also very warm and there is a real danger of sunburn.

Later Hugo and his party arrive having stopped at another Michaelis on the way. By this time the wine and ouzo is flowing and lunch is almost ready. We've realised some time ago that we seemed to be sitting in the women's section and so moved over towards the barbeque area. Here we find the likes of Yianni Rainbow, Alexis and the other usual suspects from the bar. Someone's got a bottle of whisky out and someone else tops his glass up from the water jug, which unfortunately contains Tsipero (Raki). Within a few minutes he's happily horizontal.

Yianni the teacher asks me if I can drive. Whenever asked this question I always reply 'yes… why?' Because he is catching the boat to Rhodes from Panormitis later in the afternoon (there are no boats leaving from the main harbour that day) and needs someone to drive his car back from Panormitis to the village. I consider my options: spend the day sober before driving a left hand drive car that belongs to someone else the entire length of the island or… not. I decide on not and that's o.k. we're sure he'll find someone else to take it back for him.

I ask Hugo the derivation of the name Kokimides and he's heard one story that I have probably remembered inaccurately: Many centuries ago (just prior to 1697 I guess as that's when the chapel was built) the family that lived up on this mountain were happily getting on with life. Until one day pirates invaded the island and started ransacking the place, as pirates did in those days – not Pirates of the Caribbean type pirates you understand, anyone who wanted to pillage and plunder was called a pirate. Apparently the mountain ran red with blood and everyone was killed apart from one girl who found a cleft in the tree in which to hide. The tree grew around her and she was therefore saved. It let her go again when it was safe to come out. Because of this miraculous escape the church was built and dedicated to Saint Michael; the Kokimides part comes from the Greek word for the colour red, Kokkinos.

Tales of the past are forgotten as lunch is served. We muscle in on the Rainbow table where I become particularly Greek and ask for the wine by saying (lit. trans:) 'Yianni, give me wine,' with a grunt and a nod. I become particularly un-Greek by declining the fish from the barbeque – by that time I'm full up with other goodies. The food just keeps coming. Katina, the seamstress from the village, passes out plates of all kinds of wonderful stuff and everyone tucks in. She deals with the washing up by throwing the used plates over her shoulder, narrowly missing Manolis at the grill, and smashing them amid shouts of 'oopah!'

We left before the real partying started. Word had got around that we had walked up to the party but for the return trip we had an offer of a lift. The combination of wine, sun and walking had got to our feet so they weren't working properly. As we said goodbye to friends old and new several folk tentatively asked if we were walking down and treated us like people who had forgotten to take their medication. We explained that we had a lift and everyone seemed very relieved at the news.

11.00 a.m.

Leaving Chorio and heading to Pedi by foot is a little like leaving Camberwick Green and passing through Chigly on your way to the seaside. The quaintness of the village gives way to the cicada filled, tree lined road which, in turn, gives way momentarily to the industrial area – garages and the power station, both very necessary and brief as the road soon becomes quiet and picturesque again.

The new beach (with sand) opposite Julie's bar offers free sun-beds to customers and I find Dimitris there so I have a coffee with him. Then it's time to test the new facilities and the water for the first time this year. With the sea lapping lazily at my feet and the fine sand between my toes it's easy to drift of into a dream of being on holiday. I have even disguised myself as a tourist today with cut off shirt, shorts and a back pack. I take up residence on a sun bed and observe an hour on the beach.

Soft, Greek music from the restaurant behind me, soft chat from the taverna nearby. George's taxi boat crosses the bay towards St. Nicholas and my eyes are already heavy. Last night's mosquito bites itch until I walk into the water, the cool sea calms them and me instantly. It gets warmer the longer I stay in, floating on my back as if in an isolation tank; staring up at the blue sky bleached by the sun. I hear the rocks roll beneath the water. Fish flick past. Supported by the sea I am in danger of falling asleep.

The sand dries between my toes in seconds, sandals turn hot in the sun, I move them to the shade. An occasional motorbike passes on the road behind me, a fishing boat chugs across the water, the wake reaches the shore eventually and the waves take on a new rhythm before settling back to their slow, soft lapping. The day trip boat from Rhodes crosses the horizon, far out to sea and a world away. I imaging the frenetic activity of the harbour – and instantly forget about it.

The bus has come and gone. I will have to walk back.

2.00 p.m.

I'm sitting outside the bar "working", it's early season, hot and it's the start of the Siesta hour.

Georgeos and Maria taverna has a few lunchtime guests. I am drinking soda water with a fresh lemon squeezed into it, rebuilding my strength as I embark on another 12 hour working day, three at the bar and the rest, later, at the newly opened Windmill restaurant. I am determined not to drink alcohol until after the shift is over.

George, from the taverna, comes past, stops, says: "One wine for me, one beer for you." There is no arguing and refusal would offend. He nips next door to Lefteris' kafeneion, three steps up to where Nicholas the cobbler eventually brings him a pair of sandals from his shop. The shoes are tried on over a glass of ouzo while the wine I have poured turns warm on the table. Serious footwear negotiations ensue.

The last of the day-trippers who made it up the steps to the village for a quick look and some lunch, finish their double Greek coffees and head on down, buzzing with renewed energy.

Damianos calls in to check out the Greece Vs Australia friendly football score but the TV is off – it's probably for the best.

Soft Greek music from the kafeneion next door, wood pigeons in the distance, shoe talk continuing.

A lone tourist, young, blonde, pretty – somehow separated from the herd, is drawn into the shoe mêlée but refuses a drink the old men try to press on her. A general, cross-generational and one-way flirting session ensues, much to the young things' bemusement. And when George starts singing to her, both her confusion and embarrassment mount.

Memories of the Italian (and other nationalities') occupation come in useful to the two older men as they fall into less *flirtive* chat in Italian and some English and a few Greek words thrown in for good measure.

She leaves. They leave. The wine remains undrunk and I'm in the beer trap, just having another small one, when Yianni – the teacher who lives upstairs – comes and sits, bringing fresh chick peas for us to nibble on.

We start reading our books in the quiet of the siesta hour and the square becomes a library. Shhh…

06.00 pm

We are sitting outside the shop on the Kali Strata discussing ideas for next year and watching the world go by on a hot August evening. I make notes for 24.

A huge, modern sailing yacht with grey sails taut in the wind glides towards the harbour below. The wind is picking up. Next door to us Hanna is having a new roof put on her house - a drill whines away sounding like a maniacal dentist at work, luckily it's working on wood not teeth.

Two smartly dressed Italian ladies trot down the steps in a flurry of language and colour.

Dust and leaves whip up in a small whirlwind depositing debris in my eyes and ouzo; I can't hear my music which is being played on a CD in the gallery upstairs. A fishing boat makes its way towards Yialos from Nimos, cutting a long white wake in the deep blue water. The maniac dentist on the roof is now hammering as persistent flies bite my ankles and more people pass. They are watched indifferently by the cat who sits on the wall a few steps down.

A speed boat speeds in over the waves that the wind is now whipping into small white crests. I can't hear it but I can see it bounce as it apparently attempts to break some record or other.

Panormitis passes, his ankle now fully restored, news is that he will be dancing again soon. Neil and I talk about books we are writing and having published in paperback. There is also the possibility of a photo book. A winter project.

Some young people run down topless - the boys - as sweating tourists make their way upwards towards the village square, driven on by the thought of cold beers. Some stop and browse the shop and I think of how it was years ago with twenty five thousand people living here. We chat to visitors who all comment jokingly that we have a 'hard life'. We smile politely and make the appropriate comments - if only they knew. Seven days a week in this heat, eleven hours a day before shopping, cleaning the house and taking care of the garden. I'm not complaining though.

A couple of Russian painters pass, covered in paint; a French mother and her daughter browse; a few English people stop and chat and a local Symiot comes in for some identity photographs. People visit the gallery and admire the view from the balcony - living art - as well as the art on the walls.

The cat still sits, still and contemplative on the wall below, until it finally moves off to somewhere more interesting. A taxi boat heads out from the harbour, it must be nearing seven by now, the last pick up of the day. Clare and Bonnie stop to say hello, Bonnie is as excited as usual and won't stop chatting until she's had some petting.

We enjoy the view, aware that soon a house will be completed on the corner of the Kali Strata by the bar and the view will be lost forever; we should still be able to see the sea though. A boat so small that I can hardly see it but can just see its wake is now cutting slowly through the greying sea as the light starts to fade. The waves of the wake ride the swell in humps and I am reminded of a black and white photo of the Loch Ness monster.

A distant church bell, it is the day of the Assumption today. A Turkish Gullet comes in under motor, no sails on its tall masts. And pieces of roofing timber are being carried in next door. The roof dentist has stopped work for the day. The clock in the harbour quietly chimes seven.

HOW TO MOVE TO A GREEK ISLAND
(Or another place in the sun)

A short guide based on experience

By James Collins

INTRODUCTION

- ✓ Have you ever watched one of those television programmes about moving abroad and thought: 'I wish I could do that!'?
- ✓ Have you ever found yourself dreaming about living your life on a sunny Greek island instead of in your two-up two-down in the rain?
- ✓ And have you always known that this was only a dream and would never happen because you did not know where to start?

It's not possible is it, just to give it all up and go? Not at your time of life, not with the mortgage, the job, the security. Where do you start? How do you do it? What if it goes wrong?

Well the good news is this:

- ✓ Yes, it is possible.
- ✓ Yes, you can do it.
- ✓ No, it needn't stay a pipe dream.

And no, you needn't give up your security and cut off all ties with your current life.

This book will tell you how you can make your dream come true with limited risk and maximum adventure. Obviously, everyone's personal circumstances will be different but that doesn't matter. Whether you are a successful businessman with a £50k a year income, unemployed or retired, the principals and processes are the same. And the message is the same.

If you want to do it, you can do it.

On the Greek island where I now live, I meet many tourists each year. They all have similar questions and most have the same look of wonder in their eyes. 'Do you *live* here?' is often the first question. The reply I want to give is, 'no I commute, it's a long way from Barnes but it's worth it.' But of course, I don't say that. I usually reply, 'yes I live here, now.' And there then follows a conversation about how lucky I am, how jealous they are, how they wish they could do the same thing and so on.

And the next piece of good news is this:

In order to change your life and move to your dream location you only need one thing:

- ✓ The desire to do it.

This guide lists the most popular questions people ask me and the replies I give them.

BEFORE LEAVING

Why?

This is probably the most common question. Actually, it is several questions in one word. When you tell people that you are thinking of moving abroad they often ask, simply, why?

Everyone's answer will be different. From 'because I want to,' to 'why not?' My answer is equally simple but perhaps a little less vague: 'Because I didn't want to wake up one day and think, "I wish I'd done that when I was younger."'

But when people ask 'why' they are also asking:

'What made you leave home?'

'Why here?'

And they are very often thinking, but won't ask you, 'what are you *running away from?*'

To take the last point first: I saw it as running *towards*, not away from. You may have a reason to leave your homeland which does have something to do with escape and that's a valid reason to move. To escape the rat race is a common reason, to escape from the nine to five, the weather, and the pressure of life in your country. There are many things to run away from. But:

TIP

You are actually running *towards* something:

You may still have to work, there will always be weather and there will be a different set of pressures. Expect things to be different but similar. For example, in my first year I worked during the tourist season.

BEFORE & AFTER:

Activity	Before (Back in England)	After (On Symi)
Commuting to work	One hour by car	Half hour walk down hill
At work	Eight hours. Five days a week	Nine hours. Seven days a week for six months non stop
Commuting from work	One hour by car	Half hour walk up hill, plus an hour or so stop in village Kafenion
Weather	Wet, cold occasionally warm	Sometimes over 40 degrees, sometimes too hot
Weekends	Work on house, run a company	No such thing in the season. Seven days a week for seven months

In the second year, however, due to a house sale and other major decisions I spent seven days a week every available day of the year promoting symidream.com, writing books and running web sites. (And working in the village kafenion from time to time.)

What made you leave home?'

To this question I reply, 'this is home.' If you are serious about making this move then you must accept that 'home' will be wherever you are. You may refer to your country of origin as home for the rest of your life but then you will not have made the break. This does not mean you must fully embrace the country you chose to live in, join up for its army or renounce your passport. Just be prepared to accept that, once you have moved, your home is wherever you are. After all, home is where the heart is, or wherever you lay your hat if you are a Paul Young fan.

TIP

Home is something you feel.

House is something you live in.

Where do I start?

There are a million and one reasons why people want to give it all up and live abroad. We can't examine each one individually but each one is a valid starting point. The fact that you are asking where to start proves that you are at least interested in starting. And that's a good start.

The process is this:

- Step 1   Decide that you want to do it
- Step 2   Decide how you are going to do it
- Step 3   Do it

'Sounds very simple, but I bet it isn't,' I hear you mumble. The theory is simple but your own set of circumstances will dictate how complicated the process will be.

So, you start by deciding that you want to go and live abroad. Where?

TIP

There is a big difference between being on holiday and living in a place.

Just because you had a nice holiday three years ago in Florida doesn't mean that it's the place to live for the rest of your life. Some people get holiday and life confused. If you are living abroad you are not necessarily going to be on holiday for the rest of your days. There will still be bills to pay, things to be done, chores, a routine, a rat race of a different breed. When going on holiday you take luxury money, just enough clothes for two weeks (and maybe another case full just in case,) insurance and many photographs. And you know that you are time limited. This is very different to living in a new place, a new culture and trying to establish yourself as a member of a community, as you will see.

Ask yourself what is the perfect location for you? Maybe it is somewhere that you have visited, maybe not. Either way you should research not only the country but also the exact location that you are heading for.

I want to live on a Greek island.

Which one? There are hundreds. Will you need to work there? Are you able to work in the country of your choice? Will you need work permits? Can you live there on your passport or will you need visas? There are many things to consider and you need to take a planned approach.

So, you have decided where you want to go to and have gained some knowledge about the country, area, city, or island. What next?

When is the right time to move abroad?

When the time is right for you.

I did it when I was 39. My ambition was to be living on a Greek island by the time I was 40. For some people a good time to make the break is when they are young, before children and mortgages take over. For others it is when the kids have grown up and they have some capital behind them. For others it is when they have retired and have a pension to live off. And for some it is when the children are just about to start school, promotion is in the offing and there couldn't be a worse time to uproot and change their lives.

Probably the best time to do it is when you find yourself wishing that you had done it years ago. That is, before it really is too late.

Some people I have met, who now live 'abroad', came on holiday and never went home. That's one way of doing it. It's not the easiest way, certainly if you have ties to where you are now. If you are serious about making the break then I would suggest that some sort of planning in advance would lead to more success in the future. If you are the kind of person who is able to pack a bag, get on a plane and simply not come back then you don't really need to be reading this. But do carry on because it's quite entertaining.

But you have a mortgage, you have a job, you have commitments that you need to get out of and loose ends to tie up. Obviously, you need to see to these first.

But, if you set a date, a target, you will find it much easier to get these other obstacles out of the way.

TIP

Set yourself a goal.

By this time next year I will be in a position to move abroad.

A timescale is the best way to fix the goal. By giving yourself a limited time period you will be defining your ambition and will have something to aim towards. As you get nearer to the date, you can go one step further and book an airline ticket. I suggest booking a one-way ticket. Once you have done that you will know that you are serious.

And you will have set yourself a period of time in which you must attend to the 101 other little things that must be done. Things like:

Do I sell my house?

TIP

You don't have to make a choice between security and ambition.

If you own a property in your country you don't need to sell it to move abroad. It could be rented out and thereby provide you with income while you live out your dream in the sun. If you would prefer not to have the ties that property, mortgages, tenants and repairs bring then sell it and invest the capital. You may generate enough income to live off while you are away. But if you do sell bear in mind that you may not be able to get back on the housing ladder if you return in the future.

The best advice here is to ask some questions and seek professional advice where necessary. Only you will know the best way forward.

Renting out your property

- **?** Will your building society allow it?
- **?** How much rental income will it generate?
- **?** Will you be liable for tax on that income?
- **?** How much are the agent's fees?
- **?** What do you do with your possessions?
- **?** Will storage cost money?
- **?** Are you prepared to have strangers living in and possibly wrecking your house?
- **?** Can you insure it while you are away?

Selling your property

- **?** Are you sure you won't need it again?
- **?** Will this provide you with income?
- **?** Do you need to sell it?
- **?** Are you prepared to sell everything you don't want to take with you?

TIP

If you do sell and find yourself with a lump sum:
Put it away and don't spend it!

I have met many 'ex-pats' who did just that. They sold up and went for it. They lived like millionaires for the first year and then... Oops! Savings gone it's time to live like paupers, trapped in a foreign land with very little money and no way of re-establishing a life back 'home'. Do this by all means, but enjoy your 'holiday' before you run out of capital.

Similarly, keeping a property and renting it out also brings problems. It's always at the back of your mind, what if something goes wrong? What if you can't rent it out and the mortgage isn't paid? What if property prices fall? You will be constantly aware that you have a concern in the country you left behind. If you are happy with this then keep it and do what you can.

There *is* a compromise. Moving abroad doesn't have to be such a final thing. You could give yourself a year or two's grace. Keep your property, your ties, and reconsider after a set time period. By then you will have had the chance to see if you have made the right decision without severing your ties to what was once home. You can always go back to sell the house. Unless you are moving to the other side of the world, in which case it might be better to sell it before you go.

So **'what do I do with my property?'** is not a simple question to answer. Your property is probably your biggest asset and it's not a thing to be gotten rid of on a whim. Consider your options, plan and make an informed decision.

And if you don't own a property? Then there's a lot less for you to worry about! Check out your tenancy agreement, make sure you give the right notice to quit to your landlord, pay up the rent, fix those little things you damaged, give it a clean and there you go.

TIP

Get a written reference from your landlord.

If you are a tenant of a private landlord, a housing association or a council you should ask for and be given, a written reference. Make sure that this states that you paid your rent on time, or in advance and that you were a good tenant. (Assuming that you did and you were.) Even in a foreign country this reference can prove useful. And if things don't work out and you end up coming back, well it will be useful then too.

While on the subject of accommodation: If you don't have an address to move directly to and will be looking for accommodation once you arrive here's another tip:

TIP
Book a holiday.

You may find it cheaper to book a two-week, package holiday to your destination and then not use the return ticket. For the cost of this you will get your flight and accommodation. Once there you can base yourself at the holiday accommodation while you start asking around for a long term let. Even if you don't find anything suitable during your two weeks you will have time to make alternative living arrangements while you continue your search. At least you will know that you have somewhere to go for that initial period.

Make sure you tell your holiday rep, or company, that you are not going back though.

Don't use this approach if you are taking the contents of your house with you, they might not like it at the hotel.

How much money do I need in order to make the move?

This, too, will depend on many things. Do you have a job to go to? Do you know how much rent you will need to pay? Have you researched the cost of living in your new country and so on? Again, research and planning is the key.

<u>Some things to find out before setting yourself a budget:</u>

- **?** How much is an average rent per month?
    - Take enough money for six months rent plus an additional two months rent in case a deposit is needed.
    - Also, remember the cost of utility bills and setting up a house. Unless you are moving all your pots, pans, kettle and duvet with you. Have enough to see you through until you establish a regular income stream.
- **?** What is the cost of living in the country?
    - Explore the Internet. Many places have local sites and chat rooms and you can talk to people who are already living there.

This is the best way of finding out the details of what to expect both financial and in general.

✺ Check out potential medical expenses, do you wear glasses, will you need to pay for dental work etc.

? How much will it cost to get there?

✺ If you are taking just one rucksack and a one way flight it should be cheep enough.

✺ If you are taking a van full of possessions and pets on a five day overland journey it will be a little more costly. Remember pet passports, customs controls, weight restrictions (on the vehicle not you,) motorway tolls and ferry tickets etc.

✺ If you are having everything shipped out by a specialist carrier, shipping agent and/or removal firm the cost will vary depending on how much you are moving, how it is to travel and what you insure it for. Get quotes but don't always go for the cheapest. And read the small print. And make a detailed inventory (with a Dictaphone rather than by hand, saves a lot of time.) And watch while they pack it up. And count the boxes. And check their inventory. And find out the route. And who else will handle it on its journey. And expect some things to get broken. (Actually ours went without a hitch and only one paper lampshade got squashed. But you never know.)

? Do you need to buy anything particular for the move?

✺ For example: A laptop computer so that you can write novels, listen to music, watch DVDs and so on.

TIP

When you have added up the cost, add a further 30% at least.

Be prepared for the unexpected.

Notice that I suggest taking enough money for six months. If you are moving to a place and will need to work when you get there, then bear in mind what kind of work it might be. I suggest six month's money because, on my particular Greek island, the work is seasonal. There is plenty of work in the summer but during the winter there is no work at all. Actually, I had enough money - I thought - for ten month's unemployment. It lasted for only six. *And* I was being careful.

If you have a job waiting for you when you move then you don't need to worry so much of course. Your individual circumstances will dictate how much 'back up' you need to have. The point here is to be prepared and if anything, over-budget.

How do I give up my job?

'I resign,' usually does the trick. It worked for President Nixon so it should work for you.

The problem with giving up the job isn't how you do it, it's thinking about doing it that usually stops it happening. Should I/shouldn't I? What if? How will? And all those concerns will keep you awake at night all the time you deliberate. If you have set your target date, you can work backwards from then. I suggest a period of four weeks between giving up the day job and leaving the country. This is your getting finalised period. And you will need it. Particularly as you will be, in effect, also moving house.

Changing jobs and changing house are two of the most stressful things you can do. Don't do them on the same day. You don't need to. Plan to finish work with enough time to finalise your moving. After all you are not just moving house you are moving country.

Think of this:

It is a Monday morning and the alarm clock has not gone off. You wake up wondering what is wrong. You're going to be late for work, the boss will shout at you; you'll have to stay late to make up the time.... calm down and think again.

It is Monday morning and you did not need to set the alarm clock. Nothing is wrong. You have no job to go to. You have set aside money so that you don't need to work for a few months. You can do whatever you want to today and no one will shout at you. Lie there in bed and plan what you are going to do with your day. Maybe you will check out the Internet and learn more about the place you will be soon living in. Maybe you will learn another Spanish verb, or start on that Teach Yourself Italian book. Maybe you will make that list of things you want to take with you?

Whatever you do with your first day of freedom, enjoy it. You have just come one step closer to realising your ambition.

TIP

Ask yourself: 'Can I afford to give up the day job?'
And then ask yourself: 'Can I afford not to?'

What loose ends do I need to tie up before leaving?

Another minefield but one that can be divided into two halves: (**how many other halves could there be?** Don't be pedantic. When you live in Greece you realise that every whole has at least four halves, each quarter has six parts and each part is a whole unto itself.)

Practical things and Personal things

Practical things that might have loose ends flapping about:

Your house

Selling it or renting out will produce a myriad of odds and ends to deal with. (See above if you've eagerly skipped to this part.)

Bank accounts

You can be a foolish virgin and take your cash with you in a suitcase and hope it arrives at the same airport as you, or you can be a wise virgin. Open a bank account in your chosen country before you leave – if you can, or keep an account in your present country until you are sure you are not coming back.

Either way you will need access to your money. Most places in the world these days have ATM machines. This is the best way of accessing your savings until you set up an account in your new country. If in doubt, take enough in traveller's cheques to see you through until you are established.

You may want to set up an Internet banking facility as an easy way of checking the status of your account, transferring cash etc. And you'll be surprised at how many places, even in apparently deserted backwaters, have internet access these days. Why, some even have running water.

You may need to have a contact address in your current country while you arrange new banking facilities in your new country. Check this with your bank and let them know what you are planning. They will be able to advise the best way forward. And from experience, it is no trouble at all to have a UK bank account with a non UK address.

If you're going to be getting into the 'I have a large sum of capital to invest, will put it off-shore and live off the tax-free income' bracket then check out your tax liability in the country you are going to.

Mail

A contact address is also useful until you establish a forwarding address in your new country. Once settled by your Spanish pool, or in your French apartment you can have your mail re-directed to your new residence, but in the meantime you will want to know where your mail is. The best way is often to ask a friend to accept your mail and forward it until you are settled. Then you can instruct the post office 'back home' to redirect mail for you, for a fee.

If they are really good friends, and you've promised them a free holiday, they may even filter out the spam, junk, offers of £100,000 loans at only 33% interest, gold credit cards, shoe catalogues, charity circulars and other bits of wasted rainforest before they send it on.

Medical

Have a check up, discuss any medical needs with your doctor and if necessary, ask them to write a letter 'to whom it may concern' outlining any recent treatment or an illness that may reoccur in the future.

Have a dental check up, get your eyes tested, get cracking with your osteopath and have your feet done. Do any of these things if it makes you feel better. But unless you are going to live in such a remote part of the world that health care is a) non-existent, b) very expensive or c) a lottery (like Borneo, Wadi-Halfa or parts of northern England for example,) you will probably find that some sort of medical service exists.

You may also need vaccinations. You doctor will be able to advise you about what is sensible, recommended or compulsory. These will depend on your destination in the same way as if you were planning a holiday.

Utility bills

Just like moving house you will need to arrange settlement of outstanding bills and have services disconnected before, or on the day, that you move out. Pay them. Just because you are leaving the country doesn't mean you will never be coming back and huge, multi-million pound companies who are owed money tend to bear a grudge for a very, very long time.

Email

You may wish to have a web-based email provider that you can access from any Internet café in the world until you are settled. Then you will be able to connect in the usual way using that country's providers. Provided you can get a phone line. (You may need a contract for your rented property to get a phone line.)

Insurance

You are not going on holiday so holiday insurance is not appropriate. If you come from the United Kingdom and are moving within Europe then you should start by taking an E111 form that you can get from the Post Office. (Or whatever the current arrangements are.) You can use this, in an emergency, until you are set up in the 'National Insurance' scheme of your new country. Wherever you are coming from and going to you should check out what medical insurance that country offers its residents, as you will be a resident and not a tourist. If in doubt about medical insurance, check with the local consulate or embassy before you leave or as soon as you arrive.

House and contents insurance will be a different matter and you'll need to talk to local brokers when you get there. If there are any.

Passport

Probably the easiest thing to overlook but the most vital. Without this you won't even make it to the departure lounge at Gatwick. Do you have one? Is it valid? How long for?

Again, speak to the consulate or embassy if/when your passport needs to be renewed and you are not in the UK. In Greece, for example, it involves filling out a form that the embassy/consulate sends you on request, providing the usual photographs and sending a fee. The fee takes the form of a 'postal order' and the post office provide this once you provide them with the money. They also send it on for you. The last time I did all this, the Embassy in Athens was very apologetic, explaining that passport processing was taking a very long time. Maybe as long as one month! The form was sent and the new passport was returned (to our remote island) within three weeks. They've obviously never used the English system.

However, don't leave it until the last minute. Nothing in Greece happens in a minute.

Visas

Do you need anything to enable you to stay in your chosen country for a period of more than three months? A phone call or a visit to that country's embassy or consul is the best way to research possible restrictions.

Personal things

A few other, more intimate matters, that might require your attention

Wills

You have the will to go but do you have a Will to leave behind in case you 'go' while you are gone?

It is always a good idea to make a Will if you own a property, anything of financial or sentimental value, or even just money in a bank account. You should have a Will no matter where you live, but you may need to change it before leaving to reflect your new circumstances.

Also think about how they will get you 'home' if you pop your clogs in Holland, go in Goa or kick the bucket in Phuket. The cost of shipping your body back to your desired, final resting place must be thought about. You may want to be buried/cremated/scattered in your new country, in that case check out if it will be possible and if you need a local executor to deal with it all. And don't wait to do this. Not everyone lives into ripe old age or has the luxury of 'dealing with it later'.

Family and friends

You may want to tell them what you are doing, promise to keep in touch and let them know when you have an address. Don't expect them to come and visit you though, no matter how many say they will. Out of every fifty people who promise to visit you in your new life, only one or two will; unless you're extremely popular or an easy touch for a cheap holiday.

Personal possessions

Unless you are taking everything with you, be prepared to let some things go. Sell what you need to or store what you can't live without until you can send for them. And bear in mind the cost of storage.

TIP

Be prepared to accept the conditions that you are going to live in.

That is:

If you are going to live in a remote part of India you may not have access to the kind of medical services you are used to in London. If you are going to live on a far away Greek island you won't have central heating in your house which was designed to be cool in the summer and a large fridge/freezer in the winter.

When you choose to change your life you choose to accept the changes that go with it.

Summary

- ✓ Decide that you are going to make this move.
- ✓ Decide where you are moving to. Even if you plan to travel around for a while you should at least have a rough idea of the direction in which you are heading so that you can buy some sort of ticket out of your current country.
- ✓ Set a date to leave.

- ✓ Start saving money or make sure you have fall back finances. And make sure they will be accessible once you leave 'home'.
- ✓ One month before your leaving date (at least) finish your job and start your final preparations.
- ✓ Make those preparations, tie up loose ends and check out your medical and technical requirements.
- ✓ If you do not have a property to move directly to then book a hotel, or holiday apartment to use as a base while you search for your dream house.
- ✓ Pack those bags.

GETTING THERE

Ok. I'm on the plane heading for my new life in the sun. What should I expect?

The unexpected leaps to mind.

Obviously, what to expect depends on where you are going, whom you are going with and who you are. But among the many variables there are certain things that will be the same. You are, to a certain extent, heading into the unknown.

Be prepared for surprises

You may arrive at your dream location to discover that it has changed. Where once there were open fields, sandy beaches and blissful isolation is now a nightmare of holiday hotels, golf courses and nightclubs. If you have done your research this should be less of a shock, but be prepared to change plans if you decide that you don't like the place after all.

Don't get stressed out

As I have said, moving house is stressful enough; moving country won't be any less stressful. There are many things you may not know:

- ? The culture
- ? The location
- ? The language
- ? The people
- ? The way things work – or don't work
- ? The price of a reasonable rent, cost of living, essential bills
- ? Where is the bank?
- ? Is there a bank?
- ? Who to trust
- ? What to eat

The list is endless. Take it as it comes, stay calm and enjoy the initial part of your adventure.

Beware the Ex-pats

Moving to a new community is a little like starting at a new school. Worse, it's a boarding school. Even worse (for those of us who've been through that particular system) you are only a first year and will be until at least year twenty-five.

The smaller your new location the more intense the hierarchy. I don't mean to tar every Ex-pat with the same brush but you do need to watch out for some. Here are a few stereotypes based on experience, observation and what other first-years have told me. Sadly, having re-examined the list, I seem to have developed a rather jaundiced view:

- **The chairperson**

Sadly, one of the first people you will meet will be an Ex-pat who thinks he or she is the chairperson of the intimate society you have just joined. You may be invited to dinner or to the club and that's charming. But beware of the political minefield you are being led into. Some people actually take pride in bagging the new boy. (Eugh.)

- **The wanna-be chairperson**

This will be the first person who sidles up to you, buys you a drink, welcomes you to the neighbourhood and then starts, in the same breath, to slag off the person who bagged you first. (Difficult to avoid.)

- **The keen drinker**

Unless you are one yourself and intend to flitter away your life savings on Stavros' Gin and Tonics, liquid lunches and hangover cures, try not to get drawn in by the drinking set. You may get to know people, find that the price you pay is less than the tourists do and suddenly discover that Stavros is your new best friend, yippee! But in effect all you are doing is wasting money, ruining your liver and showing the locals that you are just as lazy as 'the rest of them.' (Tempting.)

- **The National Enquirer**

This one will interrogate you subtly to start with: interested to know all about you, where you came from, what you will be doing, who you live with, what do you think of so-and-so, how much money do you have, can I tap you for a loan, (you see where we're going with this?) did you know about... Did you hear that... By the way I should avoid... He's got a shady past... she's bonking... that's not his wife... I heard that...

And when you say goodbye they move on to the next English speaking person they happen upon and pass down the line everything you just said. Only they add a few embellishments for effect and before you know it, you're a gaol-bird on the run with a Moroccan drug dealer who's running arms for the contras. (Scandalous!)

✖ The Montague
He had a fight with that English bloke six years ago and they've not spoken since. He won't let his kids go near the family and thinks they should be run out of town. He's bad news and you shouldn't go near him mate. (A bad egg.)

✖ The Capulet
He had a fight with that English bloke six years ago and they've not spoken since. He won't let his kids go near the family and thinks they should be run out of town. He's bad news and you shouldn't go near him mate. (Another bad egg.)

✖ The moaner
You'll soon know who this is because you'll be wondering, within minutes, why they ever came to live here in the first place. And why they don't move on. (Tedious.)

✓ The helper
No hidden agenda, just wants to be friendly, help you settle in, lend you a kettle until you buy one. Invites you to dine, gives you a house warming gift and their phone number for day and night use. Usually treated with suspicion by the others in her class. (A good egg.)

✓ The historian
Has lived there for years, even before electricity and telephones were in use. Has an active interest in the local area and history. Has a passion for learning the language and knows every local person of note. Is invited to church and house parties by the indigenous population and knows how the system works. Probably the most useful person to keep in with. (Star attraction.)

✓ **The unaffected**

Someone who just gets on with their life. Enjoys their chosen surroundings, accepts the local ways, ignores the gossip and the made up scandal, works hard, has fun and appreciates what they have got. (To be aspired to.)

That's enough of that.

<u>So in summary:</u>

You will receive all manner of advice on how to do this and that, who to avoid, where to eat and so on. My best advice is to make up your own mind. In many small 'foreigners abroad' communities walls not only have ears but they now have mobile phones and know how to text. Everyone will know your business, sometimes before you know it yourself and everyone will be keen to discover who you are. You will be taken under some very political wings and must be careful of who you choose to be seen with, dine with or even talk to. Sad but true.

Many will offer useful advice and many will be genuinely interested to help. You will soon get a feel for who you like and who you want to listen to. It's up to you but remember: just because you are all in the same boat doesn't mean you have to like your fellow passengers.

Bide your time, keep your eyes open and your mouth shut while you learn the lie of the land.

Respect the locals.

If you are moving abroad to experience a new way of life and a new culture then embrace it. Be prepared to adapt to local traditions and respect the local ways. If you really want to 'fit in' to your new surroundings then you must be prepared to become part of them and not just a part of the existing Ex-pat community. This is not easy, particularly if the local language is one you don't speak.

Discover where the locals hang out, what they eat and drink and how they behave and then try it yourself. It will take the locals a while to realise that you are living there and not just on holiday and slowly they will take an interest in you. This kind of thing takes time. But you have the rest of your life so don't expect to be part of their community over night.

Will I need to know a foreign language?

In a word: Yes. Nai. Oui. Ya. Si. Mam. Ja.

If you speak English and you go to live in, for example Greece, then you should speak Greek. Or rather: why should you expect the Greeks to speak English to you? Actually many Greeks (and other nationalities) speak English and are keen to practice what they know, but you should not rely on this. Before leaving 'home', it is wise to take some language tuition. It is not only polite to learn the language and use it, but necessary. If you are on a two-week vacation then you can get away with a phrase book and hand gestures. But you are going to live in this place for some time. Surely you want to be able to talk with your neighbours, explain to the doctor what is wrong or even just buy half a kilo of tomatoes?

Learning a new language is not an easy thing. You can spend your evenings pouring over textbooks and remembering verbs but the best way to learn a language? Listen, understand, repeat, learn to read and write all over again.

TIP
Learn your new language.

Ok smarty-pants. How do I do that?

<u>Think of it as building a house:</u>

Select your plot of land:
Learn the alphabet, and any diphthongs, accents, stress symbols, characters etc.

Lay the foundations:
Learn the grammar, boring, dull, tedious but vital.

Put up the brickwork:
Expand your vocabulary, adding a few new words each day.

Put in the windows:

Watch local TV, read the subtitles on films, use a dictionary to translate the newspapers, magazines etc. Listen to the language being used. The first stage of fluency is to understand.

Add a front door:

Take private lessons from a native speaker.

Add a back door:

Use what you know in the local café, bar or shops. And don't be afraid of making mistakes. To try but fail is better than to fail by not trying.

Decorate your house:

Listen out for local sayings, expressions, idioms and the finer points of the language. And use them.

Live in your house:

Speak to yourself in the language. If you don't now something then look it up, ask your teacher or try out what you think is right. If you are wrong, someone will correct you.

It is a long process.

You will not achieve it overnight but the more you try the quicker you will learn. Be patient, be thorough and persevere. It will be worth it in the end when you wake up one morning and realise that you just dreamed in another language.

How will I find a place to stay?

I take it you mean 'a place to live'? If you want a place to stay then check into a hotel, if you want a place to live in for five years or so then you need to do one or all of these things:

1) Contact a lettings agency
2) Ask around the locals and ex-pats (but beware of owing favours to people you don't know)
3) Look in the local papers

The legalities of taking a long term let will vary depending on what country you are in, what part of that country, who the house belongs to, and if you live in

Greece, what the owner's mother had for lunch on the day you viewed her property.

Whether you view properties via a lettings agency or whether you find somewhere by word of mouth there is a list of things you should have with you. Be prepared, write your list in advance and don't feel foolish when you bring it out and check things off. Some ideas to get you started:

Technical things to ask your prospective landlord when viewing:

- How much is the rent per month?
- How often will the rent be increased and by what amount?
- How long is the lease?
- How much is the deposit?
- What bills, if any, are included? Rates, taxes, water etc.
- Do I have exclusive use of the property?
- Does your mother always use the oven to bake her bread in *every* morning? Or is just today?
- Is the house connected to the mains water, does it have a well? If so is it clean and is the water drinkable?
- Does the house have electricity and gas? Where are the meters? (Take a note of the numbers when moving in or out. And keep ongoing records.)
- What furniture is included?
- Are there any restrictions on use? Can I have pets, visitors parties etc.?
- What repairs am I liable for?
- What will you - the landlord - give me in return for the rent? Exclusive occupation, decoration, external repairs etc.?
- Does the house belong to the person who is renting it to me? (Sounds daft but you never know!)
- Can I install a phone, satellite dish, TV aerial?
- What notice to leave do I need to give if/when I want to leave.
- Will I owe any outstanding bills from a previous tenant? (Check out this kind of tenancy law with a local solicitor if you can.)

If using a letting agent also ask:
- What extra fee is involved?
- What is their input once you are in? (Will they act for your in disputes etc. for example.)

Personal things to consider:

- ? Is it the right size for your needs?
- ? Does it have what you wanted? A view, outside areas, inside toilet etc?
- ? Can you afford it?
- ? Is the location what you want? A house up on the top of a cliff with stunning views may seem ideal but can you manage the 600 steps up to it? Will it be too windy in the winter or too hot in the summer?
- ? Does it have enough furniture? Too much? Is there anything else you need that the landlord should provide?
- ? Does it feel right? Can you imagine yourself staying there for a few years?
- ? Who or what are the neighbours? (Ruins surround our house, it's very quiet but for the goats, chickens, church bells and stray cats. That's preferable to the main road and motorbikes further down in the village though.)
- ? Does it have a postal address or do you need to collect mail from the post office two miles away?
- ? Ditto, location to shops may be an issue.

Write down anything else you want to know or consider before you go and view properties. If you don't speak the language, try to take along someone who does so that there is less room for misunderstanding.

Another way to find a property is to ask the local Ex-pats. Very often they will know of someone who is moving on, moving away or who has just died. But don't be afraid to ask local people either.

Should I buy a house abroad or should I rent?

Again, this will depend on several things:

- ? Your budget - can you afford to buy?
- ? Your intentions - how long are you planning to stay?
- ? Would it be a good investment?
- ? Would you be able to sell it in the future?
- ? Are you allowed to own property in that country?

The best advice on this subject is to seek local legal advice. Different countries have different laws concerning buying property. But no matter the country, there is still a common principal:

Owning a property brings security *and* commitment whereas renting a property allows flexibility but less security.

Actually, that's a bit of a misconception. Just because you rent a property does not mean that you have less security. You should have an agreement with a landlord that is enforceable under law. Just remember that the law will not be the law of your 'homeland' but of your new country and you may not be aware of all the details of the law or the language it is written in. But some kind of law will apply whether you are buying or renting. Again, local legal advice should be sought. Don't just rely on word of Ex-pat mouth here, everyone's opinion and experience is different.

What will I need to know about work permits and other legalities?

You will need to know as much as you can about all this.

When you have a place to live, you may need to earn some money. Before you set off on this adventure you did check the position with the embassy didn't you? Good, then you will know the *country's* legal position re workers from abroad coming in and taking local jobs. However, the *local* view of this may be somewhat different.

Before taking on any kind of employment you should check out certain things. See what sounds familiar about this list:

- ❓ What are the hours and days that I will be working?
- ❓ Do I need a health check? (Some establishments insist on health and safety medical checks, books and permissions. To work in restaurants for example.)
- ❓ Does the employer pay my national insurance?
- ❓ What are the wages and when are they paid?
- ❓ Is there a contract?
- ❓ Am I paid if I am ill?
- ❓ Am I insured?
- ❓ Do I get tips or does the 'house' keep them?
- ❓ Is this a minimum wage?

? Do I need to speak the language?
? What are the working conditions?

What is familiar? These are just the kind of questions that you may ask at any interview in any part of the world. Just because your new location is your dream location it doesn't necessarily follow that your new job should also be part of that dream. If you need to work then you need to work in a job that is beneficial to you, safe and properly paid. Having said that, remember that wages in your new country may not be the same as those back 'home'.

TIP

You are not only living in a different country but in a different economy.

Wages should be relative to the cost of living. Find out what the locals earn and expect/demand the same. You can't demand the same wages as you were getting as an English bank manager if you are now a foreign waiter. But you can demand the same wages as a local waiter if you are able to do the same job. Your prospective employer may use the 'you don't speak the language' excuse to offer less money. In this case, either look for another job or learn the necessary parts of the language. If you are going to work in the seasonal, tourist jobs then speaking your native language can actually be a selling point.

SETTLING IN

Well done! You are there, you have a place to live and you have an income. What do you need to know now?

What about pensions, tax, national insurance?

If you have an income and your new country demands income tax then you must pay it. This should have been part of your interrogation of the Embassy staff before you left 'home'. If not you can check this situation out with a local accountant or solicitor. If you have an income from your house back 'home' then you may also have to pay tax on that.

If you are working abroad then you want your employers to pay your national insurance, or equivalent and you may want to check if this will be recognised by your home country should you ever return. Similarly, you want to check out what happens to your contributions back 'home' before you leave. Will they be frozen, or will the contributions you make in your new country count towards the same pot?

In many places you will be required to register with the local police station or town hall. Do it. It's not because they want to keep an eye on you, or because they don't trust you or because they want to deport you. It's because, if the Police know you are there and give you permission to work there, then it is very difficult for anyone else to tell you otherwise. If you are registered at the town hall then you should be eligible to vote, receive national insurance or be flown to a hospital by air ambulance, God forbid!

What about medical problems?

Just as you would do if you moved house back home, when you move to your new location you should sign up with the local doctor. Find out where the surgery is, where the dentist can be found and where the nearest hospital is. If you are working and your insurance is being paid then you need to make sure you have the relevant paperwork in order so that if an emergency happens you are covered. If you are not concerned about this kind of thing then I hope you have enough money to pay for private treatment should something go drastically wrong.

Find out where your local services are, write down the emergency phone numbers and keep them safe and handy. (Putting them into your mobile phone is a good idea - if you have a mobile phone. If you don't have one then don't try this idea. It won't work)

How do I keep in touch with home?

Remember, you are home! But I know what you mean. Your family may be worried, before you set off, that they will never see you again. Remind them that the world is not as big as it was and it is now easier than ever to keep in touch.

- ✓ Internet cafes can be found in the most unlikely of places.
- ✓ Posting letters often works.
- ✓ Mobile telephones are readily available and text is a good medium for short messages.
- ✓ Landlines still exist, though in some places (Greece/Symi) you must have a tax number before you can get a telephone line.
- ✓ Public phones are available in many countries and you can always call your mother if you think she is worried about you.

If you are somewhere very remote then you may want to have a contact back 'home' through which you pass and receive messages. This is good if you are travelling around before settling down. They can filter post and contacts for you. You will still need to contact them and they you, but that's where email or text comes in handy.

But do bear in mind that the more remote you are the less contact you may have with family. Letters may only arrive by boat every other week, for example. Telephones and charges may be an issue; be prepared to only be able to talk to your children once a month. (I am assuming that they are grown up and are not living with you. If they *are* still living with you then feel free to talk to them as often as you like.) Of course, there is no reason why you can't have hourly phone calls with your folks if you have the suitable equipment and finances. If you want to go down this route then make sure you have a land line, or video conferencing, e-mail or telepathic powers.

And if you can't stand the thought of not being able to pop next door to check on Dad, then don't go. It's another heavy subject but people dying, getting married, falling ill or inconveniencing you in some other way will have a different effect on you once you have moved abroad. You may not be able to rush to a bedside, attend a funeral tomorrow or get back for a wedding. It all depends on where you are. Just be prepared for this kind of thing and you'll get on just fine.

Any other questions?

Tell me more about your experience.

That wasn't a question.

Now who's being pedantic?

LIVING THE DREAM

(On a small Greek island somewhere off the Turkish coast.)

The trouble is: I don't know where you are thinking of living. Therefore, my answers to your questions can only be general. In this section I will answer your questions again but the answers will be specific to my life on a Greek island. You need to know that I came from England and stayed within Europe, though only just.

This is the personal experience; take from it what you will.

Why did you move abroad?

Because I wanted to. I am an Aries and when I get an idea in my head...

I had an ambition to be living on a Greek island by the time I was forty. Here I am. I also, as I said before, didn't want to get to old age and wish I'd done it. I adopted the philosophy that, even if I came back to England after a few months, at least I would have tried. Therefore I could not fail.

When was the right time for you to move abroad?

I had actually given up my well-paid, managerial job in housing eighteen months before moving away. I spent a year in freelance work so as to save up the necessary money to make the dream happen, borrowed the extra and set the departure date for my (and my partner's) anniversary. It seemed like the romantic time to do it, as we were doing it together.

And yes, it is easier if there are two of you. Two incomes and two heads are better than one. But both of you must be on the same wavelength. You must both be sure it is the right thing for both of you.

Did you sell your house in England?

Not straight away. We decided to rent it out and try our new life for at least a year before deciding to cut the ties. We arranged rental of the property and storage of things we didn't want tenants to break, use or sell without permission. The house generated almost enough income (after servicing its debts) to pay for the rent in Greece, but also attracted maintenance and tax bills.

After a year we were faced with a choice: to go back and get into the rat race again or to sell up and stay here.

We're still here, there's some money off a shore somewhere and anything we wanted to keep was delivered by a shipping company in as many pieces as it left England in. Now we worry about the most trivial things because there's nothing else to worry about. In fact, I often worry about *not* having anything to worry about. My partner says I'm a worry.

How much money did you need to make the move?

More than I first thought. Always over-budget and then add some. There will be many unforeseen expenses. Buying things for the kitchen, buying clothes for the summer, setting up a house, buying heaters for the winter to name a few things we'd not thought of. (We brought winter clothes with us as we arrived here at the end of the summer, but when summer came we needed a lighter wardrobe.) There was also the cost of tying up the loose ends in England, legal bills, settling accounts, storage and so on. Detailed planning is the key.

Now I know you're going to ask for figures because that would be very practical. But not if you're moving to Spain three years after this was written and the world economy has gone bananas. The equation should be:

a) *(R + C+F) − (I) = (PM)*

b) *PM x S = T*

c) *T + 30% = dream*

WHAT?

a) Find out a rough idea of a local rent (via internet/phoning an agent etc.) = ***R***

Find out and add a rough idea of the cost of basic living/bills etc. = ***C***

Add an amount you want to have for fun things = ***F***

Subtract your expected monthly income (from work, investments/pension etc.) = ***I***

	This will give you a monthly total that you will have to save up in advance = **PM**
b)	Multiply that by the amount of months you intend to stay (if for a trial period) = **S**
	And this will give you a total for your 'safe'/trial/initial period = **T**
c)	Add at least 30% and go to the top of the class

And if that doesn't work, use common sense.

How did you give up your job?

Took a deep breath, spoke to the head of personnel and took the plunge.

What loose ends did you need to tie up before leaving?

For those of you who were paying attention these were listed in detail above. For the rest: it took about two years from initial decision to getting on the plane at Luton. We had discussions with the building society, arranged our 'contact' for mail, set up a web-based email account, checked the banking situation, talked to the embassy about work permits etc., looked at maps, read books, talked to people (while on holiday on the island), drew up lists, added up figures, sold a few things, talked into the night, took Greek lessons, gave them up, started again, bought more books, talked into the early hours, listened to advice, rejected it, watched TV programmes, found tenants for the house, did a few medical checks, updated the Wills, and finally, bought a one way ticket each to Athens.

Did you take out holiday insurance?

Someone wasn't paying attention. We were not going on holiday! We took E111 forms and as soon as we could, registered for IKA. (The Greek equivalent of national insurance.) Our Greek employers paid our IKA as they should have done and after working for two summer seasons, we are entitled to winter unemployment money. We are also in the 'national health' system now.

What did you expect to find?

The unexpected. And we found it. We're still finding it.

Did you need to know a foreign language?

Yes and no. Many people get by without knowing Greek. We are still learning the language and will be for many years to come. It's challenging, frustrating and at times, embarrassing but we will get there one day. Occasionally I find myself saying something in Greek without having to think about it. Many times now I find I understand what people are saying but cannot yet join in the conversation. It takes time.

How did you find a place to stay?

This was done by word of ex-pat mouth. Someone knew someone who knew someone who was moving on. After moving in, getting to know 'the locals', being seen to be living here, working hard and trying to use the language we had many offers of alternative accommodation. Word got around that we were good tenants, paid up on time and looked after the house. The next time we needed to move (after deciding to stay permanently we wanted a more permanent let,) we asked the local Greeks first. We have a better property now at a more affordable price

What did you do about work permits and other legalities?

We asked other English people who were already living here, married to Greeks or who had first hand experience of the local bureaucracy. Everyone gave a different answer. In some parts of Greece you still need a work permit even though I have a European passport. Bureaucracy is rife and it's advisable to check out local island politics on the matter before assuming that you don't need this or that. I started with the police station who sent me to the town hall who sent me back to the police station via an accountant and so on. But you get there in the end.

Did you buy a house or do you rent?

Rent. It's easier, cheaper and we can leave when we want. If the landlord wants us to move he must give us reasonable notice, and he will because we're nice.

What about pensions, tax, national insurance?

Our IKA is being paid. We need to file a tax return every March and our UK pensions should not be affected by our change of location, because we are still in Europe. (Disclaimer: you can't hold me responsible for the UK Government changing the advice they gave when I spoke to them on this, check it out before you move – things change.) Of course, in order to register for all of this we needed to spend two days on a different island, queue up for hours in the equivalent of a DSS office, borrow someone's accountant to sign papers for us and chase paperwork for a year and a half. But that's Symi for you.

What about medical problems?

We live on a remote island. We have three doctors, a dentist and a hydrofoil that visits for nine months of the year on a weekly basis bringing all manner of specialists with it. If we are seriously ill then the doctor will send us to the nearest hospital either by ferry or helicopter. The cost is covered by our IKA payments. It is quicker to get from this island to the hospital twenty miles across the sea than it was to get an ambulance to take me from our old house in Brighton to the Sussex General one mile away by road.

How do you keep in touch with home?

Look I keep telling you, this is home! But: Email, letters, phone calls. Even my mother has discovered text now. In fact we probably keep in touch more now than I did when I was living in England.

AND FINALLY

I am aware that not everyone who has bought this little guide will be moving from England to Greece and that some of the information may not be relevant to you. Also I am aware that regulations change and certain pieces of information may by now be out of date, which is why I stress that you should make your own enquiries and not rely on me to do your homework for you.

But wherever you are now and wherever you want to be then, take from the above what you will, the principals are the same:

- Dream
- Decide
- Plan
- Prepare
- Depart
- Live

© J. Collins/Symidream.com 2004

The author and publisher of this guide take no responsibility for the accuracy of the factual information at the time of your reading it. It was accurate at the time of writing. The guide is based on individual experience. You should always make your own enquiries where legal and financial matters are concerned. If in doubt contact your embassy, solicitor or other expert advisor.

Many thanks to Terri for finding all those unnecessary, comas, in the proofing, and for Neil for letting me use his contributions.

If you enjoyed this little book you can read more of James and Neil's adventures on www.symidream.com

Printed in Great Britain
by Amazon